Power Up Brilliance:
Lead from the Middle
with Courage

Merom Klein PhD

Louise Yochee Klein PsyD

Courage Institute International

Published by Courage Institute Press,

Baltimore MD USA

Tuval Israel 20136

US Tel: +1-215-529-8918

Israel: +972-4-3721008

Special discounts are available for bulk quantities or special use.

For information, please contact Courage Institute International

Please visit Courage Institute International's website @ www.courageinstitute.org

ISBN: 0989553507
ISBN-13: 978-0-9895535-0-6

DEDICATION

This book is dedicated to our cousin, Leah Moshkowitz, born in Hungary, raised in Czechoslovakia and tested in ways that none of us (thank G-d) can ever imagine. After Auschwitz, Leah brought her special spark of brilliance to Israel — to bestow love and joy, hope and pride, artistry and hospitality and courage on her children and grandchildren and on all of us who have been touched by her smile.

ACKNOWLEDGMENTS

Thanks to Professor Rod Napier, co-author of our first book, *The Courage to Act,* for sharpening our thinking about the 5 Activators that power up brilliance to "ask the tough questions," as he often says, and to design deliberations that equip teams to profit from the answers. We're indebted to Rod for decades of friendship and encouragement, for his sharp wit, and for all we've learned from him about how leaders mobilize teams to switch on their collective imagination and stay true to their ideals and principles.

Thanks to our editor, Connie Kallback, for believing in us — and reminding us how important it is to activate courage in the workplace, and provide an antidote to the fear and complacency that holds too many people back. Thanks for sharpening up our writing, and getting us unstuck.

Thanks to the many clients and colleagues we've quoted in this book – both by real name and pseudonym. And thanks to the many clients and colleagues whom we couldn't find a way to work into the narrative, but whose brilliance has been a shining example of what is possible when imagination is switched on and when partners are mobilized to step up, reach out and create new inflection points.

Thanks to our close friends at Kibbutz Tuval, Har Halutz and Shorashim, in Israel. Thanks to Dr Howard Lubert and our friends at Keiretsu Forum Mid Atlantic for powering up brilliance to see what entrepreneurs see when they bring forward new discoveries. To Dr Steven Krupp and our former colleagues from Key Management Strategies. And to Ron Resnikoff, Dr Andrea Zintz, Jim Geier, Joe Dougherty, Ciaran Beary, Dr Richard McKnight, Richard Aldersea, Mike Eldon, Smadar Tadmor, Kobi Rosenberg and other practitioners who have incorporated our work on courage and on brilliance into their practice, given us feedback and enriched the 5 Activators in the process.

And, finally, thanks to our daughter and son-in-law, Dr Elana Fertig and Dr Ben Fertig, for the brilliance to carve out a career that is rich in Purpose, energizing in Will, open to Candor, steeped in scientific and ethical Rigor, and Risks to do what needs to be done, rather than what is easy, obvious or convenient. We are so enriched by who you are and what you do.

CONTENTS

ABOUT THE AUTHORS

Dr Merom Klein and Dr Louise (Yochee) Klein are business psychologists who equip leaders to Power Up Brilliance, accelerate innovation and achieve breakthroughs when they launch new products, new organizational structures and new workflows.

They serve as Co-Directors of Courage Institute International, which was founded at Kibbutz Tuval, Western Galilee Israel — before exporting their work on the 5 Courage Activators to Courage International Business Advisors, USA.

Merom earned his PhD in Organizational Psychology at Temple University and Louise (Yochee) earned her PsyD in Clinical Psychology at Widener University, both in Pennsylvania USA. Merom, a native of Philadelphia USA and Louise (Yochee), a native of Victoria BC Canada, moved to Israel in 1998 and founded the Courage Institute.

Their clients include a who's who of healthcare and life sciences enterprises, global technology, financial services, chemical, defense and manufacturing enterprises — and an array of entrepreneurial companies both in Israel and abroad. They have also worked with NGOs and with civilian and military government agencies in Israel, Canada, Europe, the UK, Africa, Singapore and the USA.

More details about the authors and their consulting enterprise are available online @ www.powerupbrilliance.com

Preface:
Choose Brilliance, not Fear or Complacency

In a survey conducted by IBM (2010), Fortune 1500 CEOs were asked to name the most important success factor — the quality they seek most in up-and-coming leaders in their corporations. Their answer? BRILLIANCE. To get out in front of the competition and invent something new, before it's a "me-too." To break free of past trendlines and create a new inflection point that profits from innovation. To see around the next corner and get out in front of problems, so there's a clear path forward to accelerates progress. Most CEOs bemoan the fact that brilliance is in "short supply." They worry that a shortage of brilliance can subvert everything they do to invest in innovation and prosper in a turbulent and complex marketplace.

We agree. Yet, in most companies that engage us to Power Up Brilliance, there's already a cadre of really smart people, with advanced degrees and great ideas, high hopes and aspirations, good values and a solid moral core. In less than 30 minutes, we can ask a few probing questions and see them light up, show us how well they understand the business and what they'd do better if they ran the place.

The shortage of brilliance isn't caused by a lack of connectivity or visibility. Technologies link everyone to everyone, with or without an appointment or an invitation. Boundaries and silos have been replaced by matrix structures and cross-functional ad-hoc assignments. Reward systems recognize breakthrough contributions. Succession planning systems scan the environment for people who have the insight and initiative to be promoted from within and moved from one team to another.

Take yourself as an example. You know your stuff. Your heart in in the right place. You know what questions to ask. You're curious, or you wouldn't be reading this book. You see the opportunities to step up and make a difference — in the market, the science or engineering, in investment scenarios. You see the risk factors that can block or limit success. You know where conventional tried-and-true techniques can take you — and when it's time to hit the reset button and push beyond the obvious answers. Quite often, you know exactly what needs to be done.

So, what keeps *you* from stepping up and speaking out? What makes reluctant to probe deeper, wrestle down the risks or seize the most promising opportunities rather than the safe or easy ones? What keeps you from acting on what you know, not just whispering about it at the lunch-table or at home with family or friends? Or for standing up for the values and principles you believe in? For half of us, it's fear. For others, it's complacency. Both of these mute brilliance. Like yours.

Not that anyone could blame you for complacency. After all, you already work long hours and find it difficult to balance work and home. You've seen people rewarded for playing it safe, getting permission, waiting for directions, not overstepping their authority. You've seen them promoted by telling higher-ups what they want to hear rather than advising them properly. You've seen teams settle for mediocrity, following the same routines and achieving the same safe incremental improvements, without creating an inflection point or changing the game. You've seen experts confine excellence to a narrow well-defined sphere, where they won't rock anyone else's boat and won't have to step out of their small insular world.

Fear? It's rampant, both in your company and when you compare notes with friends who work elsewhere. You've seen people get fired after they stood up and spoke out. You've seen luminaries ridiculed for daring to reach higher, think out of the box, ask tougher questions, bring in new perspectives or turn up the heat — before there is a crisis to address, an accident to fix, a competitor to catch. You've seen careers red-lined when they reached for the stars, set the bar high, and faced setbacks pursuing goals that everyone knew were ambitious and difficult. You've seen evidence to validate the Japanese proverb, "The nail that sticks out is the one that gets hammered down."

If you're in the C-suite, we understand your ambivalence about your CEO's call for brilliance. The last thing you want is a hoard of luminaries who misinterpret the call for brilliance as a license to go rogue. You want leaders who have good peripheral vision as well as depth and foresight. To see how their initiative and innovation affects others around them. And to know when it's time to hold their ideas in check and support someone else's success, because even a well-capitalized corporation cannot fund everything.

Take RIM, now Blackberry, as an example of brilliance gone awry. If you ever visited RIM's headquarters during their heyday, you'd be blown away by the brilliance they brought into their small company town in Western

Ontario. If you ever called them for technical support with a thorny or complex problem, you saw how hard-working and dedicated they were. There wasn't a problem they couldn't solve or an idea they couldn't develop, no matter what hurdles they faced. Brilliance? In each individual silo, they seemed to have all they needed — and more.

Yet, as an enterprise, they failed to co-operate and see the opportunities that Apple and Android, Microsoft and Motorola seized. Without a miracle, they might be out of business or a minor player by the time you read this book. "What went wrong?" the business analysts and Blackberry's devoted customers asked. Was it a belief in their own invincibility, the narrow perspective that comes from living an insulated life in a small company town, where you spend more time looking inward rather than looking outward at the competition and the market?

From everything we read, heard and experienced about RIM, the company had lots of small-b brilliance and lots of individual and even small-team courage, but couldn't harness it to get all of the lights switched on in the right sequence to create a bigger-than-my-silo win. They couldn't generate "luminous efficiency" when one group sparked another. When teams came together, former employees reported that they fought and stifled each other's brilliance and eroded each other's courage — resulting in residual heat and stalemates, rather than game-changing brilliant, leapfrog-your-past innovations. People learned to keep their heads down safely below the political parapets, do their prescribed jobs and not make waves until "the coast is clear." They played to win, rather than playing to lift each other higher and power up everyone's brilliance, rather than making my lumens outshine someone else's. The results were tragic and each of those individual units is now being split up and sold, at a significant discount.

Why, you might ask, does someone at your level need to know how to overcome fear and complacency and Power Up Brilliance? After all, isn't shaping a brilliance culture the responsibility of the CEO, the board or the executive team? Quite right, it is. And, if they're serious about innovation, breakthrough results and thriving, not just surviving, in turbulent complex business environments, they will ask the right questions and see when to pivot in a different direction. They will design reward systems to incentivize Big-B Brilliance, rather than little-b fiefdoms. But even when a CEO sees what needs to be done, there's only so much that any C-level executive or board member can do. There's only so far they can reach, in flattened hierarchies, complex matrix structures, fast-paced interdependent teams, virtual and distributed collaborations, partnerships and global alliances. There's only so much they can dictate, when the problems to solve and the opportunities to seize are incredibly complex and require everyone's brilliance, not just a few elite luminaries at the top. There's only so much that they can do to set the tone, when so much of what shapes the culture is below their sight line and outside their physical or social media reach.

In a world of flat, complex matrix structures and global alliances and networks, those at the top sound the call. They provide the oxygen and the fuel. Beyond that, we *all* take a turn lighting the spark and igniting brilliance in our local teams, one encounter, email exchange or meeting at a time, rather than letting fiefdoms and politics, mediocrity and fear dummy us down. We all have the power to get people powered up — to ignite (or stifle) the brilliance that luminaries have the potential to bring forward. Starting with what we do with our own potential. What we call "corporate culture" is a mosaic that we each create, every time we have an opportunity to lead from the middle — to step up, reach out and ignite the potential brilliance within and around ourselves.

So, if you are part of the 99% who is *not* currently in the C-suite or board meetings, this book is written for you. Because brilliance is not a spectator sport in a flat team-based, matrixed and interdependent enterprise. If you know what opportunities are golden — before there is broad-based support — nothing will happen if you sit on what you know. If you stay safely within your silo when you Power Up Brilliance, you could achieve some stellar local wins but sow the seeds of the next Blackberry. Yes, it takes courage to stay engaged in a dialogue where you receive fierce opposition, rather than folding and muttering, "Whatever." It takes an infusion of your energy and passion to rally a team that is comfortable and satisfied with its past efforts, but isn't yet doing enough to compete in tomorrow's market. It takes influence, not authority, to accelerate a project, as the lynchpin and glue that's orchestrating a multi-departmental, multi-business unit cross-functional matrix effort. It takes guts to accept accountability knowing that you do not have control of everything required to achieve success, especially if something goes wrong on your watch. And, with all this talk about power, results, accountability and acceleration, it takes patience and sensitivity to recognize when someone is too fearful or complacent and to step up, reach out and embrace or awaken brilliance.

In a 30+ year career advising leaders on business transformations, we've seen some incredible brilliance. In 20/20 hindsight, it's easy to say, "WOW," and be awed by what they accomplished. When we read about countless others, in books and articles about visionaries like Steve Jobs and Dov Frohman, Tom Larsen and Ed Rendell, King Sejong and Queen Rania, Joseph-Armand Bombardier and Robert Collymore, Joseph Neubauer and Frederick Banting — and countless other giants — it's easy to buy into the illusion that someone at the top gets "the big idea," pulls the strings and gets others to simply go along for the ride.

But ask anyone who's worked inside a system that was mobilized to go faster, further, deeper, leaner or in a totally different direction from what was ever been done before. In these success stories, and many others, the real brilliance came from the midde-out and the bottom-up, not just from the top-down.

- Underwriters achieved a 700% reduction in insurance claims — because *safety (or, in insurance parlance "Loss Control") engineers* looked deeply enough to see what upgrades would protect worker safety, and then built business cases and withstood pointed, sometimes personal, criticism to get underwriters, account managers and operations managers to act on their recommendations.

- Physicians achieved a 250% improvement in surgeries completed without complications — because *nurses* stepped in, reached out and spoke up when they knew what needed to be done, before they saw the month-end statistics.

- Product leaders brought 500% more New Drug Applications to the

7

pipeline — because *computational and analytic chemists* stepped up and challenged the thinking of medicinal chemists, rather than acting like a service group who were content merely analyzing and reporting on the compounds they were given

- The regional VP won a new bid that delivered $2 million to the bottom line at a 50% higher profit margin — because *foodservice managers* shaved a few percentage points off of their margins in order to be part of a multi-service contract that included foodservice, engineering, janitorial and security services.

- *Highway maintenance managers* stood up to social pressure and bullying when their efforts to power up brilliance and improve productivity were resisted by union workers who opposed the Governor's plan to achieve a 30% productivity gain.

- *Research directors* improved the formulation of a new gene therapy and improved efficacy in the clinic — by seeing what would solve vexing scientific problems and taking the lab work in a totally different direction from the one that the founder and inventor insisted was right.

- *Marketing and pharmacoeconomics experts* were a step ahead of shifts in the marketplace and had to convince commercial and franchise managers, who had hegemony, to rethink their reimbursement and patient-compliance strategies and reduce profits in order to keep the product on formulary

- *Business development teams* resurrected abandoned early-stage products from corporations that lost interest — and found outside investors and development partners who would help turn those products them into valuable assets.

- *Young entrepreneurs* decided to stay home, rather than emigrate, and build enterprises in a young fledgling economically distressed country under attack — and built the ecosystem for their country to become "The StartUp Nation," a global hot-spot for innovation and entrepreneurial growth

- *Department heads* knew that technology upgrades or outsourcing — while right for the enterprise — would mean that they would be laid off and agreed to bring those improvements online before they shut down their own operations.

Each of these successes — and countless others — were created because leaders in the middle chose to power up brilliance rather than indulging fear or complacency. None of them were blind or immune to the adversities, competition, narrow-mindedness, politics, technical and adoption hurdles that had to be faced and overcome. But they weighed the options and decided to take the high road — and bring others with them.

In our previous book, *The Courage to Act* (Klein and Napier, 2003), we described 5 Courage Activators as the antidote to fear and complacency. Courage gives you what positive psychologist Martin Seligman (1998) calls "a healthy defense against reality," to see not "what is" or "what was," but what can be. Goals may be daunting, your job security may be uncertain, and your stock options may not yet be above water. People in power may not embrace your ideas right away. Courage won't change those facts. But it *will* give you the resilience you need to keep those realities from chipping away at your happiness, your principles, your hope, your mental edge. It will renew your sense of adventure. And, believe it or not, when you power up your brilliance, research suggestions that it can actually change your luck.

These 5 Activators — which flip the switch and power up brilliance — are deliberate and active choices in the face of adversity. If you can encode these responses into your reflex-reactions even when you are challenged, threatened, shouted down or crowded out — or when you need more fuel and oxygen than your sponsors have provided in their first investment traunch — we believe you can produce results that are at least as amazing as the success stories we've witnessed with other game-changers. The choices are:

- **Purpose:** Hold each other accountable for a lofty noble outcome and staying aligned behind optimal aggressive business metrics — rather than settling for what's easy and pedestrian

- **Candor:** Open each other to hear and speak the truth — rather than hearing only what you want to hear or saying only what others want to hear

- **Rigor:** Get the right people with the right know-how mobilized, deployed, orchestrated — rather than relying only on the players within your span of control or the ones who give you easy access

- **Risk:** Make a personal investment in someone else's success — rather than seeking a personal triumph or pushing others out of your way

- **Will:** Sustain and revitalize spirit and energy — rather than indulging frustration or fatigue or justifying a lack of grit and determination

Here are three radical things we've learned by watching what leaders in the middle do to cultivate these 5 Activators in real teams, real matrix structures, real business ventures and in communities under fire.

One, it takes all 5 Activators, in a fluid motion, to Power Up Brilliance. 4 out of 5 don't get you 80% there — any more than a good backswing without a good grip will get a golf ball to go where you aim.

Second, getting fluent with the 5 Activators is a skill, not a character trait.

Third, it's a skill that's contagious and that's spread by contact.

If you already have mastered these 5 Activators in the way you manage yourself, and power up your own brilliance, this book will show you how use the 5 Activators — the formula — to imbue *others* with courage and ignite their brilliance, at the points where they are too fearful, threatened or complacent to get on board. And if you haven't yet mastered one part of this formula, this book will show you how to power up your own brilliance — to transcend fear and complacency and flip the switch on your own potential, with a little help from your friends.

Our deepest fear is not that we are inadequate. Our deepest fear is that we are powerful beyond imagination. It is our light more than our darkness that most frightens us. We ask ourselves – who am I to be brilliant, beautiful, talented, and fabulous? But honestly, who are you to not be so?

You are a child of G-d. Your playing small does not serve the world. There's nothing enlightened about shrinking so that other people won't feel insecure around you. We were born to express the glory of G-d that lives in us. It's not just in some of us; it's in all of us. As we let our own light shine, we unconsciously give permission for others to do the same.   When we liberate ourselves from our own fears, simply our presence may liberate others.'

- Marianne Williamson

Chapter 1
Your CEO says, "March or Die":
Does *That* Power Up Brilliance?

If you work in an enterprise with more than a few dozen employees, you have participated in "The Big Announcement." Like the Captain of an airplane, your CEO says, "Buckle up. We are about to hit turbulence." Then your CEO sets forth a Bold New Vision, an inflection point that pivots the enterprise in a new direction to stay aloft and deliver the goods. Most Big Announcements end with a call to action, to get on board, support the change, flip the switch and Power Up Brilliance.

In the weeks or months before the Big Announcement, there's a feeling of uncertainty, anticipation, anxiety. Rumors abound. Higher-ups huddle behind closed doors in conference rooms and retreat centers, accompanied by strategy consultants, lawyers and other advisors — some of whom have a reputation for restructuring and bold moves that can turn careers upside down. Political coalitions form and reform, as people try to sense "which new way the wind is blowing" and where the power will reside in the post-Announcement world.

Small companies do the Big Announcement by ushering everyone together into a conference room. Or, they head off to a conference center, so everyone can fit into one big tent. Enterprises with a global reach may bring one group together for a live meeting, near the Corporate Headquarters, and invite others to connect virtually. If you're 10 or 14 time zones away from HQ, you may wake up in the middle of the night to hear the Big News as soon as it is announced. And see what brilliance your senior leaders have dreamed up, and what more they will ask of you.

The news everyone waited to hear

Like most CEOs, Dr C had been coached and rehearsed for his role in The Big Announcement. He strode up to the podium with a bounce in his gait and a beaming smile. He wore a crisp spring-colored suit, a lightweight sweater, no tie. He was fit and tanned.

"We are at a critical inflection point for our company," Dr C said, in a strong steady voice with an upbeat cadence. He knew that lots of rumors had circulated about the new strategy, the new structure and that people were hungry for answers. The word T-R-A-N-S-F-O-R-M-A-T-I-O-N!" appeared on Dr C's powerpoint in 5 different languages, with word art and flash animations. Using a slide deck peppered with photos and cartoons, facts and figures, Dr C showed what more the caregivers and patients, regulators and payors, investors and partners expected from his healthcare enterprise. He showed industry trends and projections. Despite record profits for the past two years, he said, the current rosy trendline was unsustainable. He Dr C presented a GANNT chart with key milestones and next steps. His message: "We have to change. Fast. We have to create a bright future, before we get caught in an undertow. We can do it, if we start now. Here's how."

To conclude with a call to action, Dr C described the biggest test of courage he faced as a military doctor. During a lull in hostilities, he ordered his unit to tear down and move their field hospital to another hilltop. "For the time being, It seemed a lot warmer and safer to hunker down and stay put," he said, "But our intelligence told us that we had to march or die. For ourselves and for everyone in our care. It wasn't easy to pack up everything and shuttle it over the ravine, 12 km east in pouring rain. But, sure enough, as soon as the rain cleared, our old location was overrun. In our company, I'm telling you that you may not hear shelling in the distance and it may feel safe and secure right now, but we also have to march – or we'll die."

Dr C's address was compelling — for the luminaries who already "got it" and saw this as their opportunity to step up, shine and make a difference. They walked out inspired, powered up, ready to shake things up and do whatever it took to get to the next hill. During the Q&A, they wanted to know when it would all begin, how they could get involved, and congratulated Dr C on his epiphany about industry trends and his vision to make their company the innovator and trendsetter.

But the vast majority of Dr C's audience was stunned. They sat, arms folded across their chests, and glared at the podium, avoiding eye contact. The Communications Director who advised Dr C on his key messaging and his powerpoints was surprised. Dr C had solid facts. He had great anecdotes. His delivery, as usual, was upbeat. If he'd been speaking to investors, payors or patient advocacy groups, he'd have received a standing ovation. But the vast majority of his troops — who were being asked to do the heavy lifting to march, not die — were threatened and daunted. Some were insulted. Despite everything Dr C said about looking forward, his

15

troops were looking backward, defensively and protectively.

During the Q&A, the holdouts were politely silent. But the Luddites —
who were angry, not passive — unleashed their wrath after the town hall
meeting, on blogs and social networks. They branded Dr C as a reckless
daredevil, out of touch with operational and pragmatic realities. They
defended their track record and extolled past accomplishments that Dr C
trivialized as "business-as-usual." They refuted Dr C's facts and figures.
They accused luminaries of kissing up to the boss and throwing them under
the bus. "Some opportunity," one cynic wrote, "to destroy our company
and derail our careers by promising the moon to investors and chasing an
elusive dream." They ridiculed Dr C's military record, and posted pictures
of the soldiers who'd lost their lives and limbs under his command.

Enterprise-critical innovation imperatives

Dr C was a sophisticated leader. He knew that luminaries with courage
and vision would hear the call, "March-or-die," differently from those who
seek security and routine, who avoid conflict, who confuse empowerment
with carte blanche and mistake teamwork for easy quick consensus,
kumbaya and harmony. He knew that some would bide their time, protect
their old entitlements and be holdouts or laggards, waiting until someone
said, "Yes, we're serious. Join us now. Participating in the future is not an
invitation you can decline." He anticipated that some holdouts would be
Luddites, intent on sabotaging the effort, if given an opportunity.

Dr C also knew that looking the sceptics and cynics who say, "It's impossible. It's never been done," have facts on their side. It's easier to see what's wrong with a bold new objective — or why it should *not* receive an investment —than it is to find the work-arounds. It's easy to look backward, at trendlines and precedents with 20/20 hindsight, than it is to look forward at a market niche or unmet need that no one has ever filled before. Positive psychology expert Martin Seligman (2011) tells us that optimists and visionaries like Dr C have a "healthy defense against reality" which equips them to see possibilities and inflection points that Luddites will find threatening and that lingerers will react to by saying, "Wait and see." In the face of doubt and uncertainty, courage gives luminaries strength to Power Up Brilliance, to find a way to get things done rather than explaining why it ought not be attempted — or justifying why it failed.

To equip luminaries with courage to set the pace, Dr C personally form two dozen innovation accelerators — and staffed those accelerators with a cadre of luminaries he personally selected to orchestrate change. Some of the orchestrators were expected to define micro-TRANSFORMATIONs — for a therapy, a regulatory team or a key health insurance provider that was skeptical whether to keep their drugs on formulary — in addition to their "day jobs." Other innovation teams were given broader mandates and were relieved of their old duties to work full-time on special assignments.

When we talked with Dr C about the improvements assigned to these innovation accelerators, we asked three questions: "What does success look like? Why is it a 'must-do' and not merely a 'nice-to-do?' Why now?" We set these criteria to determine whether each innovation initiative was a "Must-do," worthy of "March-or-die" or a merely a "Nice-to-do."

Merom Klein & Louise Yochee Klein

Brilliance: Nice-to-do or Need-to-do?

Nice to do Recreational or grandstanding for personal advancement Small-b Brilliance	Need to do Enterprise-critical fiduciary responsible Transformation Big-B Brilliance
✠ From SWOT* analysis, there is no clear Threat if you stay on the old comfortable trajectory	✠ From SWOT analysis, there is a clear Threat if you stay on the old comfortable trendline
✠ From SWOT analysis, the Opportunity is not supported by a robust business case	✠ From SWOT analysis, there is a clear Opportunity — supported by a robust business case
✠ If you delay, the Opportunity will still be there or will become even greater	✠ If you delay, the Opportunity will vanish as competitors move in and fill the niche
✠ If you delay, the Threat will not loom larger	✠ If you delay, the Threat will grow more damaging
✠ Morally or ethically neutral or less – does not make the world any better	✠ Morally or ethically compelling and uplifting – makes the world better
✠ Your motivation is personal — your ambitions, your visibility, your interests, your lifestyle	✠ Your motivation is fiduciary — add value for customers, users community, shareholders
✠ Good for your team or business unit but costly or neutral for the enterprise-as-a-whole	✠ Good for the enterprise-as-a-whole but neutral or costly for your team or business unit
✠ Neutral or negative impact on your enterprise's reputation in the market for core Strengths	✠ Advances the core Strengths that distinguish your enterprise from competitors in the market
✠ Requires more bandwidth than core revenue and profit generators can allocate	✠ Can be managed with available bandwidth – without eroding current core business

(* SWOT is an anagram for **S**trengths, **W**eaknesses, **O**pportunities and **T**hreats – the foundation for most strategic planning deliberations)

18

5 Power Up Activators: The antidote to fear and complacency

So here you are. You're a luminary who "gets it," and you've been tapped to take time out of your day job and orchestrate a "march-or-die" innovation initiative. You're not in the C-suite — not even close. Your office is several floors or maybe several countries or continents away from that lofty perch. But, in your own world, your own project team or your own key account, you see how the initiative you were asked to orchestrate can make a difference and accelerate "T-R-A-N-S-F-O-R-M-A-T-I-O-N." You're turned on about being recognized as a luminary. Now what?

We don't blame you for some hesitation. Dr C looked buoyant, tanned and confident when he strode up to the podium. But we heard Dr C voice his worries and concerns when we sat down with him in private behind-closed-doors deliberations and late-night phone calls. Dr C harbored no illusions. He had rivals who still resented the fact that he'd been chosen over them for an important and coveted position. He knew that his insights and ideas would threaten a few of those rivals on his leadership team, who would say politically correct things in public and would look for a way to slow or subvert his plans. Dr C understood that bold new moves make a CEO vulnerable, because they make everyone look for bold new results — in a market where just staying even with last year is no easy accomplishment.

Just as you understand that volunteering for more than the minimum your job description asks you to do is a bold move that can advance — or red-line — your career. So, like Dr C, don't go rogue and head into your Innovation Initiative alone. Get a coach — a coworker or mentor you can trust, an outside advisor, someone out of the politics and there, 100%, for you. And use the 5 Power Up Activators to get yourself mentally equipped to lead from the middle and Power Up Brilliance, at the inflection points when fear or complacency will lead in one direction — and success will lead somewhere else. The chart on Page 21 shows you the 5 Activators — the North, South, Centre, East and West chambers in a 5 cylinder engine that Powers Up Brilliance and gives you the torque and drive you need to get a big load up a steep hill and around a sharp curve:

Set your compass North — with Purpose. Where is the "next hill" that you envision for your enterprise, department, business unit, alliance or project team? Or for the client you are advising to "march-or-die?" Describe it well enough for them to see what life can be when they get to higher ground — and why it's a "must-do" rather than a "nice-to-do." Show them the end-game — and why the promise and potential are worth the danger and inconvenience. With data. Like Columbus putting together a story-board for his expedition across the Atlantic, you may need multiple versions of the Purpose to power up brilliance with multiple audiences. One might be for your sponsors, like King Ferdinand and Queen Isabella, who will finance the voyage and allow you to sail under their flag. Another might be for the shipbuilders and outfitters who will equip you for the voyage. And another still might be needed to recruit your crew — a mix of *Marranos* like you, who have nothing to lose in the wake of an Inquisition and are seeking haven in a Brave New World, and solid, experienced, competent but sceptical sailors who want to return safely to their homes with treasure.

Look South — and assess the Risk. Put a challenge in front of some hard-driving take-charge personalities and they'll push forward with

The 5 Courage Activators
How Leaders Power Up Brilliance

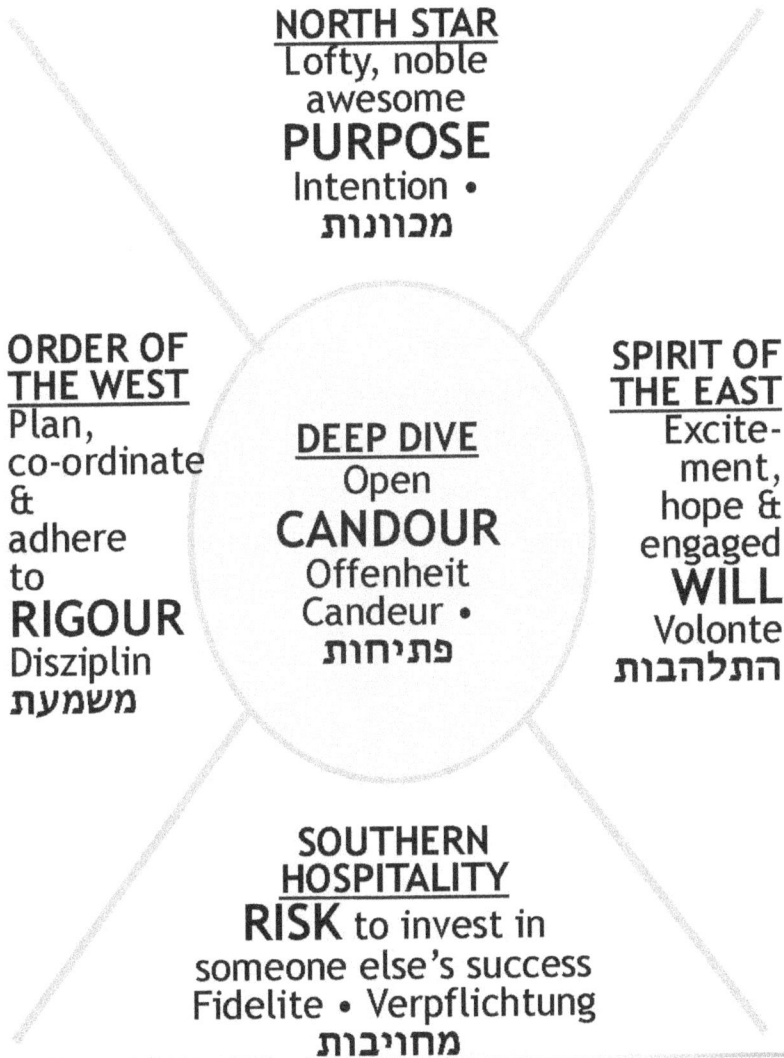

NORTH STAR
Lofty, noble
awesome
PURPOSE
Intention •
מכוונות

**ORDER OF
THE WEST**
Plan,
co-ordinate
&
adhere
to
RIGOUR
Disziplin
משמעת

DEEP DIVE
Open
CANDOUR
Offenheit
Candeur •
פתיחות

**SPIRIT OF
THE EAST**
Excite-
ment,
hope &
engaged
WILL
Volonte
התלהבות

**SOUTHERN
HOSPITALITY**
RISK to invest in
someone else's success
Fidelite • Verpflichtung
מחויבות

the power of 10,000 wild horses or a herd of charging buffalos — and do "whatever it takes" to make things happen. That's how Dr C was wired. But other personalities can be stifled, shut down, shut out by that same charge-ahead energy. As you think about the partners you'll need to recruit, you may have your preferences — but you'll need to adapt your perspective to ennoble partners who are wired differently from you. If you are a hard-charging Buffalo, like Dr C, you'll need to know how to reassure teammates who are motivated not to charge ahead but, like Protective Wolves, hold back, look around, and say, "Wait. Let's assess the danger and make sure we can protect our pack.". Danger. To the Protective Wolves, the danger is moving too fast and injuring those who need a slower pace or who need to be carried over tough terrain. To Charging Buffalos, the danger is that we'll be too slow, too plodding to "march or die." There are literally dozens of personality profiles that divide us into personality types, by color, by number, by compass direction, shape, or by 4-letter combination. The key isn't which system you use. It's whether you can round out your own personality and rein in your own frustration and indignation, when the risks you are asking of others evoke fears — real or illusionary — that you do not see. And it's whether you have earned their trust when the seas get turbulent and stormy, and you ask them to put their financial survival, career advancement, project team success, their time and budgets or this quarter's bonus in your hands.

Look deep into the Center — and open Candor. Sometimes people don't want to hear what they don't want to hear. Sometimes, they threaten to "kill the messenger" — even when you know what needs to be done and you have expertise that others should take to heart. But most of the time, what looks like a shortage of Candor is really an ineffective delivery. As an orchestrator, you may need to broaden your listening skills — to "get" what others are telling you, even if their delivery is off-putting or so low-keyed that it's easy to dismiss. And, when you deliver your "March-or-die" call to action, you may need to tailor your delivery so others get the imperative, rather than retreating in fear or defensiveness or indulging their old complacency. If you're in a direct blunt culture — working with data-driven blunt engineers, planning with Israelis or Danes, being scrutinized by Dutch, Scots or Koreans — you have an obligation, not just a license, to speak up and assert what you know and foresee. But take that same *dugri* bluntness to a group of HR consultants, to Japan or France or to an Arab village in Israel that's preserved its own culture and language and you'll be dismissed as someone rude and insulting. Even in America, regional differences dictate how Candor should be delivered so it's heard constructively. The Northwest Nice manner of Portland, Oregon, or Genteel Southern manner of Tuscaloosa, Alabama, may not be bold enough to get a native New Yorker or Bostonian to stop, look and listen. And, conversely, a New Yorker may inadvertently alienate someone from Toronto — even when the outspoken advisor issues a stern warning because "I am covering your back."

Look East — and renew your Will. According to the Native American (or First Nation) Peoples, there is an order to the world, a directionality to the forces that Activate and Power Up Brilliance. Energy, enthusiasm, spirit, wonderment — these come from the East, like the dawn of a new day or the rejuvenation of a new Spring. If you come East to Israel, you, like most visitors, will be struck by the pioneering, can-do, make-it-happen

23

fast-paced energy that you'll see before you even leave Ben Gurion Airport. Come to BioMed or to the Agricultural Show in Tel Aviv and you'll feel the buzz as soon as you enter the convention hall. You'll feel the fire in the bellies of the inventors and entrepreneurs. Decades before the Israeli currency was stable and way before unemployment was low, the energy, optimism and can-do spirit was all we had. It's what brought Ethiopian immigrants back to Zion, walking across the Sudan, sometimes mourning the loss of family members who were too frail to "march or die" along the way. It kept American, Australian, English, Canadian and New Zealander immigrants smiling and singing, rather than returning to an easier (but less fulfilling) life in their countries of birth. Does your team already have that zeal, resilience, passion, confidence, pride? Does it have the emotional intelligence to see when someone is having "one of those days," and reach out to infuse them with renewed energy? If not, it may be up to you to be a cheerleader who can get under people's wings and give them lift with a smile, a humorous quip or encouraging word — whether or not that's in your natural character to do.

Look West — with Rigor. As we said about Dr C, he harbored no illusions. He knew that a rallying call would mean nothing without execution. And that an innovation culture would take root only if enabled by reward and performance management systems, career ladders, portfolio and project management systems, matrix structures — and a thousand other tools, systems and processes, along with the skills to make the most of them. Our colleagues, Rick McKnight and Tom Kaney, recommend a "strategy map" so success isn't left the chance, wishful thinking or expansive grandiose ambitions. They advise CEOs like Dr C to charter teams who will back up grand plans with step-by-step formulas, knowledge and information exchanges, rational priorities tools and process upgrades, and the skill development that will equip team members to use new tools properly. Innovation experts like Goldenberg and Boyd (2013) and Cooper and Edgett (2012) suggest innovation maps and planning tools that do not make breakthrough innovation a matter of serendipity or happenstance, but of robust thinking with proven templates to uncover possibilities that are hidden in plain sight, waiting for you, as the innovation orchestrator, to pull them out of the team you lead.

We raise Saint Bernard puppies. A 60-kg (130-pound) dog who doesn't have a "strategy map," a "stage-gate" or an "innovation template," and who hasn't quite mastered co-ordination of those large paws and massive frame can be quite funny to watch, unless she's lumbering toward you with muddy feet and a slobbering grin. When she's got more enthusiasm than restraint, more bounding energy than grace, wrestling a big dog into a small harness can be quite an entanglement. So it is when a large complex enterprise starts to experiment with new tools and techniques to foster innovation. At first, before the moves are smooth and all four legs work together, it can seem pretty clumsy — and a lot messier than when the beast was asleep and her brilliance lay dormant. So it is with a massive enterprise-wide innovation initiative, mobilizing new cross-functional matrix structures. And with the innovation initiative you power up and lead from the middle, with oxygen and fuel from the top-down.

What to take from Dr C's T-R-A-N-S-F-O-R-M-A-T-I-O-N

If you're in the C-suite, we hope you realize that the best you can do is to sound the call and sponsor the results you need to see. You provide the direction, oxygen and fuel. You then pass the baton and rely on luminaries to lead from the middle to Power Up Brilliance and get the job done.

Like Dr C, we recommend that you articulate the Purpose behind your "March-or-die" imperative. And do your homework, to be sure that there is a real opportunity and a real threat, not just a way to indulge your ego or advance your own ambitions. We recommend that you line up sponsors, as Dr C did with most of his board members, because you'll need them to "have your back" when Luddites come out swinging. And that you find the luminaries in your team — those with the potential for brilliance — because, in almost every transformation we have seen, the brainpower you need is usually right there in your existing team, waiting to receive the call.

If you're a luminary, remember that it takes work — real work — to Power Up Brilliance. Despite your own clarity and enthusiasm, your brilliance will stretch some key people beyond the tents and hilltops where they've already dug in and created a secure, protected base for themselves. If Dr C's lofty perch as CEO — and his impressive CV — couldn't insulate him from a criticism and a wall of "wait-and-see" procrastination, why should you think you're above reproach when you step up, speak up and reach out? Or that you'll command more engagement, voluntary and discretionary effort than Dr C when you try to get people jazzed. Especially if they look at past performance, and feel they're already at the top of their game.

Like any big climb, the view from the top is breathtaking. And the stopping points along the way are exhilarating. But it's still a climb. As they say in French, "Bon courage!"

Chapter 2
The Resilience to Rebound:
How Courage Powers Up Brilliance

We feel best about ourselves when we are powered up. When we put our virtues and our talents to the test, look fear or adversity in the face and show courage. When we stand up for our principles and mobilize support, rather than keeping our heads down and taking the coward's way out, knowing that we are colluding with something that isn't right. When we achieve something great rather than something small. Each of us has these personal highlights etched in our memory. They remind us how brilliant we really are.

We admire others when they are powered up. Their courage keeps us gripped to our seats in movies, glued to the news, riveted to a biography or historical novel. From every age of human history, epic stories about triumph endure and continue to touch our hearts and our souls. We revere national heroes like Nelson Mandela, Indira Gandhi and Romeo Dallaire. We award undaunted pioneers like Sandra Kurtzig and Julian Adams, visionaries for peace like Shimon Peres and King Hussein, Princess Diana, Yitchak Rabin and Anwar Sadat. We admire executives who stay true to core values and "walk that talk," even when the going is tough. Year after year, we find inspiration in stories of freedom and empowerment — like the story of Moses, Miriam and Aaron leading the ancient Hebrews across the Red Sea and through the desert, from Egypt to Israel.

Courage – the capacity to power up brilliance in adversity – is a paradox. Intellectually, we understand the phrase that Churchill borrowed from Aristotle — "Courage is the first of all virtues because it is the one that sustains all others when they are stretched to the limit." We admire courage vicariously, when we see it in others, and feel good when the danger passes and we can talk about our triumphs in the past tense.

But, no thank you, we prefer *not* to need courage in the here and now. We'd rather have job security than a precarious or uncertain future. We'd prefer to send our kids to college to "find themselves" rather than sending them to the Army to defend our freedom. We prefer bonus objectives that play to our strengths rather than stretch goals that seem daunting or unprecedented. We prefer to keep living as we live rather than acknowledging "inconvenient truths" that demand bold breakthrough innovation. We would rather brainstorm and get gold stars for the first obvious easy ideas — rather than face a robust critique that sharpens our thinking, rejects some ideas and elevates others to true brilliance.

Complacency feels good, comfortable, secure — even though it does not Power Up Brilliance or innovation. And fear? We all come hard-wired with a fight-or-flight reflex — with an instinctive ability to sniff out danger and head for higher ground, or fight to protect the refuge we've secured. When we're gripped by fear, we're more likely to be defensive, combative or to honker down and keep our heads below the parapets — rather than Power Up Brilliance.

But researchers at Israel's Weizman Institute have discovered a small region of the human brain that switches on whenever we draw closer to the things we fear and engage, examine, interact, observe and innovate — as what they called "fearful *non*-retreaters." The sub-genual anterior cingulate cortex (sgACC) — or, as they called it, the "Courage Center" — can literally override the reptilian and mammalian brain centers that trigger a fight-or-flight reaction. It's this higher-level cerebral brain that equips us to stay calm, calculating, rational and keenly observant — even when what we fear makes us want to close our eyes, scream and run away.

Why should you know about the sgACC, if you are leading an innovation initiative that does not involve cutting-edge brain research? To rest assured that the partners who are threatened by the change you ask them to embrace — and refine — also are hard-wired the capacity to sooth their fear, quiet their outrage, look reality in the face and Power Up Brilliance. All you have to do, as a leader, is to flip the switch.

"Courage," Prime Minister David ben Gurion said, "is special knowledge. It's knowing *how* to fear what we ought to fear and how *not* to fear the things we ought not to fear." How to fear and not fear starts with the decision to flip the switch within yourself, and engage rather than withdraw. And then to reach out and power up someone else's brilliance and make it contagious. Here are a few examples.

The onset of the tsunami

On one mid-September day, within hours of the news that Lehman Brothers had collapsed, the financial crisis hit one $500 million publicly traded corporation hard. They had nothing to do — even peripherally —

with Lehman, but were caught in the aftershock. "At first we thought our computers had gone down," a European VP recalled. We asked, "How could this be? In customer after customer, standing orders went from tens of thousands of Euros per month to near zero, literally overnight. It was like one of those mystery movies where you log on in the morning to do a routine transaction and find that all of your accounts have been closed or cleaned out. We didn't believe it. We called our IT department to verify that the systems were working. Then we called our customers and were shocked to find that they had, in fact, cancelled so much of their business."

Like any tsunami, this one arrived in waves. It hit Europe first and then, in rapid motion, spread West, over the ocean, to hit the Americas. Overnight, the entire global corporation lost 35% of their projected sales volume for the year. Their two largest customers teetered on the brink of bankruptcy, carrying millions of dollars of receivables.

Their stock price dropped in days — from $29/share to $5/share. Before the tsunami, most of the members of the Management Executive Committee (MEC) were millionaires. Now much of their personal wealth was gone. Would the stock price go lower? Would it ever recover and get them above water? No one had a crystal ball.

We don't often think of a CEO as someone who has to lead from the middle — unless we've walked in those shoes. But, in the aftershock of the tsunami, this CEO felt pressure from all sides. Some of his shareholders were panicking as the analysts warned that things could get bleaker. Some panicked quietly. Others spoke up and wondered whether they made the right move promoting this CEO and allowing, perhaps even encouraging, his predecessor to retire. Perhaps, a few thought, it's time to divest — while we still can salvage some value for our shares.

The CEO was also getting heat from the bottom-up and the outside-in. Customers wanted assurance that the company will continue to ship and deliver on time, to spec, with existing — or better — service and support. Suppliers wanted assurance that their bills will be paid. Associates wanted to know if their livelihoods and futures are secure. And those in the C-suite wanted to know what to say and do both at work and at home. In the midst of the crisis, gripped by fear and uncertainty and overwhelmed by the complexity of it all, it's natural to revert to our mammalian "child-to-parent" instincts — and look to the CEO to give us the answers and make everything OK.

Taking command: Pull the team together — with candor. It was the European Managing Director (MD) who remembers calling the first emergency MEC meeting, before the CEO could grasp the scope of the tsunami. In our previous book on *The Courage to Act* (Klein and Napier, 2003), we said that courage is built before you need to test it in a crisis. So it was here. The MD knew he could step in, reach out and take charge to mobilize and orchestrate a meeting — and that he would receive support rather than resentment or political jockeying for overstepping his authority. His message was simple. "Houston, we have a problem."

Talk about "how to fear what ought to be feared." If you had this CEO — and his team — hooked up to the sensors at Weizman Institute on that emergency conference call, you'd see the sgACCs in their brains light up like Times Square on New Years Eve. With so little cash coming in and so much still being spent to on daily operations, there was no doubt that something had to give. They had to figure out it out and act – fast. And had to do it rationally, lest they set a panic in motion that would make their shareholders, customers, suppliers and their best and brightest associates run for higher ground.

The most important thing that the CEO could do, when he was awakened by the announcement of an emergency MEC call, was to set the tone, not issue orders or dictate the answers. Think about it. To set the tone. A tone of reason over emotion, deliberation over politics, data-driven rather than opinion-driven problem-solving. It was a tone he had to set from the middle, in all directions — down the hierarchy, across to CEO colleagues outside and up with board members and shareholders who were visibly shaken and panicked.

Set the compass North — with Purpose. Lots of companies have lofty Destination Statements and Core Values hanging prominently in their lobbies and posted proudly on the websites. Lots of CEOs sit in well-appointed trophy-laden boardrooms, lean back in their chairs and tell you, "People are our most important asset. We're only as good as the initiative, creativity, integrity and ingenuity of our front-line associates." This one was no different.

You don't need a MBA or a C-level title to figure out the priorities when you are digging out of a tsunami that's eviscerated your business. Secure the orders that can be secured. Retain customer loyalty. Keep competitors from taking advantage of the chaos and getting a toehold with your franchise accounts. Stop haemorrhaging cash. Cut expenses.

When you have to take action – quickly - what happens to Core Values like Entrepreneurship, Customer Commitment, Integrity, Respect and Safety — and a Destination Statement that declares, "we are the premier source of top-quality manufacturing solutions?" How do you keep people focused on the things that will continue to optimize top-line growth, value and loyalty when everyone can see that you've got to make some draconian moves and they're waiting to see where the axe will fall?

While the MEC was still deliberating — and questioning whether they would need to pivot and adjust their Destination Statement and Core Values — two things happened. It you didn't know any better, you'd swear it was just good luck that fell out of the sky and landed, unexpectedly, like a gold meteor in the parking lot. But if you were on hyperalert and were paying attention — like this CEO and his MEC — you could see they were signs that said, "Walk your talk. Stay on course. Innovate and Power Up Brilliance to do more better leaner. But don't change direction."

The first was an initiative that was started by an alert Account Manager, on his own without knowledge or authorization from a MD in the C-suite. When they heard that the company's two largest customers were about to file for bankruptcy, they knew they had to act fast. By the time the MEC came back up for air, the deal was done. The account managers maneuvered and got the company designated as a "strategic supplier." When bankruptcy was declared, this designation meant that the company would be paid first, not last — in full. The account managers understood that the business could not afford to lose $10 million in unpaid receivables. They understood the value that they provided to these two key customers, as a result of the years that they "walked the talk" of their core value, Customer Commitment. They stepped up and walked the talk of the Core Values, with Entrepreneurship and Customer Commitment. From the middle out.

When you speak with Mr B, the CEO of this corporation, he'll tell you that the "strategic supplier designation" was more than the first bold step that put their company on the road to recovery. Securing $10 million in receivables that might have been lost was a major victory. But, from the CEO's perspective, it was far more. He points to it as a key inflection point that validated their Destination Statement and Powered Up Brilliance — in the C-suite — to preserve, even strengthen, the Core Values that had been demonstrated time after time and now won them the coveted "strategic supplier" designation.

The real test of Purpose, the CEO says years after the crisis, wasn't what he personally clarified for mid-level leaders when they got him on the phone and asked, "What should we do?" It was what they did — on their own — guided only by their inner compass of right and wrong. "That's how we knew we had made our Core Values a real competitive advantage," the CEO said. "We were inspired by our mid-level leaders, possibly far more than they were inspired by us. What we had to do was to get the word out so that everyone in the company would be just as inspired by these events as we were."

Imagine that. A CEO being inspired by you and the initiative you took, when you were left on your own and had only the Core Values to guide you. In every major transformation we've seen that's been a runaway success, there are literally thousands of defining moments like this when leaders in the middle stepped in, reached out and took charge — rather than waiting for permission or direction. In Dr C's company, many of the successes never filtered up all the way to a member of the MEC. But make no mistake. Someone somewhere saw the opportunity and flipped the switch.

This sense of Purpose doesn't just happen. It's the result of leaders in the middle — one, two, three levels below the CEO — who led from the middle before the tsunami and made sure that teams embraced the Core Values, Credo, Destination Statement and by the slogans that are emblazoned on the company's website? Do you know yours well enough to do that? Could you use your own business acumen and figure out what needed to be done, even if was something different from what was spelled out in your performance objectives for the year? Would you be an example for others to follow — including those above you on the organization chart — before you were asked to do so or were reassured that you were still on the right track?

Connect East — to re-energize Will. A crisis looks different in foresight than it does when the danger has passed and you're looking back the ordeal. In hindsight, the MEC of this corporation looks heroic. Their stock is now trading at close to $80/share — almost triple its pre-tsunami value. Customers continue to be loyal — and reward the company paying premium prices for the engineering and formulation services they provide and for delivering products consistently just-in-time and fit for application. Their board is happy. They are an acquirer, rather than an acquisition target. Associates give them top ratings for creating a great place to work.

Foresight is different. "We always expected things to recover," Mr B says, "if we could keep working hard and doing what we knew how to do. But would it rebound in a year, two years, more? We knew it would take more than a quarter or two, but no one could know exactly when the orders would start coming back." The question was, would the teams they needed to mobilize — associates and shareholders, customers and suppliers — continue to power up brilliance, innovate and seize opportunities aggressively before they could see their hard work pay off.

Sustaining consistent grit, determination and extra effort is hard enough to do when you are paying people nice bonuses, contributing to their retirement accounts and their kids' college funds, when they can see a clear path to career advancement and a nice promotion. But none of those perks were available after the corporation announced staffing cuts and expense restrictions. High-potentials who had been groomed for promotion were moved back a few rungs and were now doing double-duty — producing as well as supervising, orchestrating as well as strategizing. Co-workers who had been good loyal contributors were suddenly out of work, and there was no guarantee that further cuts wouldn't be necessary, if sales continued to be soft. There was more travel, not less, and it was coach-class, not business-class, whether by train across Russia, by plane across the Pacific or by car across Ohio and Pennsylvania, Queensland and New South Wales.

Here you are. It's a Wednesday afternoon. You're eating lunch at your desk — late — because your last call ran over and there's one more to squeeze in. You glance at the picture on your desk and roll your eyes, knowing that you'll likely get home too late to tuck in your youngest child and will leave in the morning too early to see your oldest off to school. The last thing you need is some snarky email from HR reminding you that you forgot to submit some form that they need for Heaven-knows-what. Can't they see that you're flat-out with *real* work — that will bring *real* money into the company? Your phone rings. You answer it, without looking at the incoming number, thinking that it's the Procurement Manager whose call you ate lunch at your desk to catch. It's a member of your team. "Boss," he says, "I don't know how much more of this I can take. I just got my ticket for Sunday's trans-Atlantic flight. They stuck me in a centre seat — again. This is getting really old."

At defining moments like this, when you're a middle manager who sympathizes with your team member's frustration, it's tempting to demonize the higher-ups in the C-suite. But you catch yourself. After all, they're flying coach-class too and are on the same austerity program as everyone else. It's tempting to tell your teammate to buck up and hang in there — or rush him off the call quickly, so the Procurement Manager won't go into voicemail and initiate another volley of messages and emails. Or to share your own fatigue, since you're just as close to hitting the wall yourself. None of these will help. No matter how cathartic they might feel in the moment.

So you chill yourself out. (Psychologists call it "self-soothing.") You chuckle, apologize and quickly set a time to get back to your teammate. "Honest. Don't go anywhere. We'll talk in an hour. No matter what. This is important." Then you switch gears so you're on your game for your Procurement Manager call.

When you do get back to your teammate, you open the call with an upbeat greeting like, "Hey, road warrior." You put his discomfort in perspective with a reassuring, "Won't this be a war story for us to tell the kids, when they look at us with envy after the stock goes up past 60 and we're set for life." Then you get serious. You thank him for his sacrifice and discomfort. You assure him that no one could solve the engineering and application problems as well as he could, and the customer couldn't keep producing without him on the job. You make sure he knows how important he is and how grateful you are for his perseverance. Then, you offer to buy him a drink — before you remember that he doesn't use alcohol.

In the two years that it took for the company to rebound — and the two more years it took for the stock to hit $80/share — at least a hundred of these conversations took place every week. Do the math. That's more than 20,000 defining moments when a talented coworker was tempted to quit, back off or lower his/her head safely below the parapets. When it took a smile, a reassuring word, a larger perspective, a chuckle, word of reassurance that says, "I feel your pain." When tight budgets mean that you can't afford to pay for the extra effort you need from someone, all you have to give is pride. And heartfelt appreciation. You can look at your colleague, give him your undivided attention and say, "Look at me. In the eyes. Listen. We'll get through this and come out on the other side. Together." Each of these conversations was like breathing on a coal and keeping it alive, to power up brilliance.

Candor revisited — over and over and over again. When a tsunami hits and tough questions are asked, conventional wisdom tells key executives to respond, "No comment," until the dust has settled, the spin-doctors have weighed in and the lawyers have vetted and sanitized every nuance. That's safe. But it does little to lift worried people above fear and complacency — and ignite the brilliance and agility they'll need to take control of the things they can control and seize opportunities.

"Will there be more layoffs?" a manager asked anxiously, figuring that her job would be next on the block if there were another wave of cuts. The answer she received from her boss was straightforward and honest. "We really don't know. It depends how quickly our sales recover."

In 11 words, delivered with a look of empathy and sincerity, this manager communicated three key things: (1) I'll tell you the truth, even if it is not the reassuring or definitive news that you want to hear. (2) I trust you to handle the truth in a professional and responsible way. (3) Let's talk about the things we can control — namely, making the most of every revenue-producing opportunity — and not the things we can't, like the state of the economy and how far the shareholders are willing to underwrite the red ink of operating at a loss.

Sudden economic downturns aren't the only things that create tsunamis. In

Herman's company, the tsunami was a sudden and unexpected change of ownership — when his company was sold to an offshore collaboration partner, known to be much tougher and ruthless about "managing by the numbers" than the corporation who hired him.

Herman was informed of the divestiture in a phone call from his daughter. She heard it on the the morning radio news. According to the report, the deal was signed and would close within a month. The European acquirer already owned an operation that was similar to Herman's 20 km (12 miles) away and could easily consolidate the two. The ink was not dry on the deal, but the speculation was already on the news. As other members of Herman's team received calls, texts and emails, work stopped. The entire team was panicked, paralyzed, distracted. People buzzed through the office asking, "What have you heard?" and, "What will you do?"

Herman called his boss, who, of course, was unavailable, huddled behind doors with her MEC. Seeing the level of fear rise — along with complacency about the work that still needed to get done — Herman took charge. He whistled across the maze of cubicles and called his entire Department of 20 people together in a crowded conference room. He read them the news release. He took their questions. He responded to most of them with phrases like, "We don't know yet. We'll have to see. Here's what we know about the company that acquired us from their website, from past business dealings, from industry analysts." Then he redirected the focus and said, "The best way to ensure our future is to get back to work and do the very job we can. Here's what our performance data say about what we are doing month-to-date. And here's what we've got to do, to increase our enrollments."

When Herman called his team together, the fact is that he didn't know any more than anyone else in the team. But this wasn't about sharing information. Or building a strategy to onboard and join the offshore acquirer. It was about building courage. About reaching out and activating the sgACCs — the Courage Centers — of fearful, angry or complacent colleagues so they would re-engage, Power Up Brilliance and do their jobs as well as possible, which was the one thing they could control.

Connect South — when you ask partners to risk. We don't often think of "doing your job" as a risk. But when the future is uncertain, as it was for Herman's team and for Mr B's associates, it's an act of faith for key talented team members to power up brilliance and invest mentally and emotionally in the enterprise — rather than taking a recruiter's call and jumping ship to join another team. Yet, that is exactly what Herman and what every one of Mr B's managers asked of their key associates — to put their loyalty to the team ahead of personal ambitions and job security that a competitor promised to satisfy.

The success of any team effort requires us to invest in someone else's success. As the late US President Harry Truman once said, "It's amazing how much can get done if you don't care who gets the credit."

Herman earned his team's loyalty by visibly putting his associates' advancement, job security, visibility ahead of his own. Even when it was clear that the new owners were culling through the list of employees to determine who was essential and non-essential, Herman made sure that his best and brightest associates got credit for the contributions they made. He took his lieutenants to key meetings, so the new owners could see how they conducted themselves. "The best job security we have is the good work we do," Herman reminded his team. "And the way we co-operate and support one another. That's all we can control. The rest is out of our hands." Herman took the high road and walked that talk — knowing, full well, that his team's brilliance and independence meant they might not need him. Putting your team ahead of yourself is what servant-leadership is all about.

You may face a tough test of trust when a colleague or a sister project team could use assets that have been allocated to you. When you can step in a close a sale today, rather than putting it in the hands of a junior staff member so that she can advance and sharpen up her selling skills. Or when someone in the MEC congratulates you and gives you credit for a success that rightfully belongs to someone else. In these and countless other moments of truth, do you choose to advance your own ambitions and secure your own position and your resources — or create an opportunity for someone else?

The corporation that lost 30% of its orders on the 15th of September asked its associates for the biggest leap of faith when the company's fortunes were finally looking up. After two years of hard work and sacrifice, traveling in coach and doing double-duty, the company was earning a profit. Rather than reinvesting that profit in the business and giving associates a bit of breathing room and support, the MEC decided to pay the shareholders a dividend. The MEC knew that most associates would not understand the rationale and would misinterpret their decision as one that "sold them out" rather than one that protected them against the very real threat of a divestiture.

It has been three years since the MEC paid that dividend. Associates at all levels and multiple disciplines still talk about "what they could have done with all that money," upgrading equipment, refurbishing facilities, rehiring talent, relaxing spartan economy-only travel policies. But the banter has a wistful rather than a resentful tone, a like someone talking about "what I would do if I won the lotttery," rather than "what was due me and someone took away."

How did this MEC earn the trust of its associates, to give them the benefit of the doubt on a counter-intuitive decision? It wasn't some damage-control crisis-communication strategy that they initiated after the decision was announced. It was because they had build trust for years before they needed to cash in their chips and ask their associates for the benefit of the doubt. When they explained their rationale for using profits in that way, their behavior was authentic and real. It was consistent with everything the associates had seen from MEC members for years.

It's easier to trust that your management is telling you the truth when they have consistently told you the truth before. It's easier to believe they will reward your loyalty with retroactive bonuses and with remuneration that "we cannot discuss or promise right now" when they have dealt with you fairly in the past. It's easier to believe that your colleagues in a sister project team, region or business unit will "have your back" and treat you equitably when they have done that in the past. And when you have built the business literacy that many associates lack in middle management and on the front lines, so they can see what you see, interpret the data as you do and understand the long-term implications of the decisions you make.

If you are a leader in the middle, like Herman, you are not just a link in a chain. You are an interpreter. The facts are the facts. But it is your explanation that gives them meaning. One careless and sarcastic quip about the CEO's personal wealth, one skyward glance or shake of your head, one selfish political manoeuvre, can undo years of trust that a MEC has built when teammates are afraid and the future is uncertain. Likewise, a consistent pattern of giving your MEC the benefit of the doubt, seeing events with a friendship rather than an adversarial lens, saying what you'll do and doing what you'll say — these have the power to create a culture where associates put enterprise-success and long-term career prospects ahead of short-term and parochial gain.

Push West – with rational thinking and templates that you are fluent using. Ask people what gets a team through a tsunami and out on the other side. Their answer will be unanimous. "Quick thinking and decisive fast action." But decisiveness can lead you astray when you are driven by fear or complacency. That does not happen when the courage center of your brain is activated. Courage does not make the fear of consequences or the looming big threats or the very real dangers go away. It simply makes them recede into the background. And allows you to sharpen your focus, pay attention to what really matters, process relevant data and screen out distractions. So you can make not only the quick decisions, but the right ones as well. Even when they are counter-intuitive, to someone who does not see what you see and know all that you know.

Take USAirways Captain Chesley ("Sully") Sullenberger, the pilot who orchestrated the soft landing we now call "the Miracle on the Hudson," after a flock of geese disabled all the engines on his Airbus 319. He laughs when he's asked, "Weren't you afraid?" and answers, "We did not have time to be afraid. There was too much at stake and too much to do."

Sully's explanation is smaller-than-life. He talks about years of practice drills, simulations, training, experience. About a crew who knew the equipment, the terrain and the procedures so well that they could spring into action and improvise without having to consult a manual or learn-while-doing. And flight attendants who knew how to read a plane-load of passengers and see who they could deputize to reach out and keep the crowd calm and orderly, thus preventing a panicked stampede. When the tsunami came, they could swing into action and rely on instincts and routines that had been encoded into their reflexes, waiting to be accessed like a MP4 that was in the library and ready to be locked, loaded and played.

When you are in the heat of a high-pressure, fear-provoking, conflict-prone situation, it's too late to think of what you should do. This isn't the time to think of what to say, how to control your gestures and mannerisms, modulate your voice tone, manage your emotions. If you are a skilled public health doctor, like Herman, you know how to call people together, calmly and with a smile, no matter how much anxiety you feel about your personal situation. If you are a retired US Marine Sergeant, you know how to bark an order at a panicked businessman — quickly — and get him to back off, sit down and make way for mothers and children to exit a disabled plane in an orderly way.

According to psychologist Gary Klein (1999, 2004, 2011), who studied decision-making by fire-fighters, emergency room physicians and other professionals in crisis situations, it is too late to list all of your options and weigh the pros and cons. You've got to scan the situation, see the patterns rather than the component parts, and rely on what looks to outsiders like intuition or gut feeling to decide what's right, take initiative and bring others with you.

As you read more in this book, we will offer you a way to activate your sgACC when when you face business tsunamis or fleeting opportunities take you out of our comfort zone. We will offer you a way to scan the reactions you get when you say, "March or die" or "We've got to act — now," and lift combative, negative Luddites beyond their reptilian fiight-or-flight instincts and lift frozen-into-inaction laggards above procrastination. We will offer you a way to mobilize support to create economic miracles and lucky rebounds like the ones that this corporation achieved — whether or not you have a seat on your company's MEC.

And we'll offer you a few templates you can use — when new business conditions, technology or regulations take you into situations that are different from the ones stored in your well-rehearsed MP4 libraries and you have to figure out what will make you successful and seize opportunities, quickly, before they get away.

Chapter 3
If You Were in Charge,
How High Would You Set the Bar?

As the orchestrator of a cross-functional innovation initiative, setting goals is the first thing you do. You want to know what will contribute most to enterprise success and what your sponsors expect. If there are multiple sponsors in a matrix structure, you will have multiple objectives and multiple interests to balance.

If you're experienced in setting goals — for departments, cross-functional teams and individuals — you've probably used the S.M.A.R.T. formula. Goals are S.M.R.T. when they take a noble Purpose and give it focus and a sense of urgency with a **S**pecific, **M**easurable, **R**elevant, **T**ime-bound target.

That leaves the "A" in the formula — how high you set the bar. Do you use historical data to plot a straight line on a graph, and use the trendline to validate what is **A**chievable? Do you look at industry trends or corporate benchmarks and set the bar at a level that is **A**verage or slightly above, with a slight stretch for incremental improvement? Do you look at operating costs and set the bar at a level that is **A**dequate to eke out a profit, pay a dividend or earn a bonus? Or do you use best-case scenarios and game-changing innovations and business models — igniting brilliance — to strive for something **A**udacious and **A**spirational, when your team members show up with their A-game and achieve breakthrough innovation?

How High to Set Aspirations?

AUDACIOUS
achieve
breakthroughs to
outperform what
anyone though
possible

AVERAGE
reach parity
with
others in your
industry/
market

ADEQUATE
achieve enough
to eke out a
meager profit

This chapter will start with observations we made decades ago — with a retail sales organization that fell on hard times. We'll see what role brilliance plays in luck, and what role luck plays in being about to achieve something Audacious and Aspirational. And we'll then bring it down to earth for you — if you're working in a life sciences, high-tech, defense or artistic enterprise where you're solving problems that have never been solved (and, perhaps, never even attempted) before.

The retail dilemma

In the mid-1990s, a prominent women's lingerie retailer in the US fell on hard times. The US economy was in recession. The US military was cutting costs, following the Base Relocation and Closure Act, and many of their most profitable stores were adjacent to the military bases affected by the closure. Add to that the demographics of aging baby boomers whose body shapes no longer were flattered by a previous generation of the company's merchandise.

Yet, in the midst of this perfect storm, some of the stores in the chain were outliers, brilliant performers that were defying the market pressures by continuing to post soaring sales and profits. "We're lucky," one of the high-performing Store Managers said. "From what I hear, the other stores in our district don't get as much foot-traffic across the threshold as we do."

That simple explanation didn't sound logical to the VP of Stores. He asked us to see what was really happening. So, we selected 20 stores at random for scientific observations. We trained observers to count the customers who stepped across the threshold and entered the stores, to see how long it took before they were approached by a sales associate, and how the interaction affected their purchases. The VP of Stores also hired mystery stoppers and gave them $500 to spend in each of the 20 stores, *if* they were approached by a sales associate and *if the sales associate* made a suggestion.

The VP's intuition was confirmed. These so-called "lucky" stores — the outliers — had almost exactly the same foot-traffic as the stores whose sales had plummeted. There was no objective difference in their "luck." There was, however, a sharp difference in the way customers were treated when they entered the stores. In the high-performing, trend-defying stores, Associates started conversations with four times more of the shoppers. In the stores where shoppers were ignored, the mystery shoppers walked around the store and left, without spending one penny of the $500 they had been given. So, we could infer, did many other shoppers.

A few days after the observations, we asked the 20 Store Managers to estimate the number of shoppers who had crossed their threshold and entered their store on that Saturday. The outliers, whose sales trends defied market conditions, gave fairly accurate estimates. But, the average Store Managers *under*estimated their foot traffic by 75%. They believed only 20 shoppers had entered their store on that Saturday, not the 80-100 whom our observers saw cross the threshold.

When we shared our data with the District Managers, they were dumbfounded. Like the Store Managers, they assumed that the brilliant stores were "just lucky." They had no idea how they were actually creating their own luck. Yes, there were things that the company could do to make it easier for Store Managers to meet their sales targets — and they did start work on a new store motif, new advertising, new fabrics and new products. But, in the interim, there also were things that Store Managers could do to transform an Audacious S.M.A.R.T. goal into one that was not just possible, but feasible, *if* it was approached with a Powered Up Brilliance.

Suppose you were a Store Manager and were asked to set a sales goal for your store. How high you'd set your "A" would depend on what you saw. If you were a Store Manager who underestimated the traffic by 75% and who let Mystery Shoppers leave without spending their $500, who could blame you for setting the bar low? But suppose you were a Store Manager who believed there were 200% more customers, and whose Associates approached, rather than ignored, the Mystery Shoppers and sweet-talked them into spending the $500 they'd been given. If you could count on that kind of "luck," it wouldn't be Audacious or Awesome to Aim high. It would just be good sense.

Lucky personalities: The link to brilliance

British psychologist Richard Wiseman (2004) did a series of studies on "lucky" personalities. Yes, he found, there are some people who have an uncanny knack for being in the right place at the right time and who, statistically, are more likely to win contests, lotteries and supposed games of chance — and who are more likely to find killer business development opportunities. According to Wiseman's research, these lucky people see things differently, whether they are managing lingerie stores, selling securities, handling household chores or leading complex drug development product teams. And, according to research by Robert Cooke and his associates at Human Synergistics, "lucky" US Army recruiters, FDA and FAA inspectors, financial services professionals and safety engineers also create their own luck by approaching things differently.

One of Wiseman's experiments brought 10 research subjects at a time into a research laboratory, all of whom had volunteered for a study of luck. The experimenters glued £50 notes into pages of the London Times and gave a newspaper to each of the 10 volunteers. The 10 volunteers were told to go through the newspaper and look for a specific BMW motorcar advertisement, and were told they would receive £5 if they found the ad. While the volunteers combed through the paper, looking for BMW ads, only two out of 10 were "lucky" enough to find £50 notes. The rest assumed they simply were not given the opportunity — rather than believing that they were so focused on the BMW ads that they'd paged right past the same rewards. Wiseman replicated this experiment five more times, always with the same result.

In his book on creativity and innovation, marketing guru Jacob Goldenberg (2013) describes five techniques that alert innovators can use to create luck — with subtraction, division, multiplication, task unification and clever correlations. In each of the vignettes he describes, to show how his clients adopted his techniques to create Audacious and Awesome luck, rather than settling for something Average or Adequate, he describes an initial reaction of skepticism, cynicism, stonewalling, naysaying. In each vignette, he describes the coaxing it took to get complacent corporate executives to try a proven, but counter-intuitive innovation methodology.

Wiseman never mentioned the word "brilliance" when he described the differences between lucky personalities and the rest of us. Nor did Goldenberg when he distinguished the successful reluctant adopters from the laggards and Luddites who said, "Not invented here," and rejected his methods. Robert Cooke used the gentle terms, "constructive and higher-level thinking" when he described the good luck that adaptive thinkers achieved vis-a-vis conventional rule-bound thinkers or power-minded, please-the-boss thinkers.

For decades, we watched some enterprises reinvent themselves, streamline and re-engineer their processes, earn incredible wealth with "wow-that's-so-obvious-why-didn't-I-think-of-that" innovations or, like the lingerie chain, keep doing what they always did but do it better, faster and leaner. We saw some extraordinarily innovative scientific teams solve pK, toxicology and CMC problems that had stymied their predecessors in another culture on another continent; and we saw highly effective safety teams mitigate the risks that previously had been accepted as "what goes with the territory" in accident-prone professions.

After decades of observation — and data from a long-delayed doctoral dissertation — we finally put it together. In an epiphany, which we then validated with our own research data, we realized that what set all of these high-performers apart wasn't just an innovation template, a black-belt in lean process mapping, extraordinary intuition, cognitive alertness, focus, and an approach to life's problems that was more can-do and optimistic rather than nay-saying and defeatist. It was how the *leaders* in these teams stared adversity, fear, negativism, opposition in the face – and responded not by going where the trendline of precedent and circumstances would take them, but by creating an inflection point that took things in a different direction. Our research and experience highlighted 5 interventions that leaders made, to lift their teams beyond Adequate and Average — to Audcaious.

We named these 5 success behaviors the 5 Activators. Here's how they played out in the culture of the high-performing lingerie stores:

Purpose. In the lingerie stores, high performers saw each visitor as someone they could assist and entice, whether they eventually made a purchase or not. They believed they were not just selling lingerie, but improving the lives of the people who visited their stores. They saw their jobs as "making a difference." They were evangelical about the higher Purpose they were serving and refused to have that undermined by economic conditions they could not control.

Candor. The high performers weren't just aware of their overall customer count. On an individual level, they listened to their visitors, open-mindedly and without preconceptions or defeatist assumptions. They used conversation-starters that engaged their visitors, rather than approaching them and asking "May I help you?" and getting a guaranteed rejection like, "No, thanks, I'm just looking." Each customer was its own feedback loop — did I engage in a real conversation or merely keep the encounter at a superficial transactional level?

Rigor. The high-performers were there to solve problems for their visitors. Make suggestions. Provide entertainment. Not only did they know what more they *should* have in their stores and lacked, they knew what they *did* have and what it could do. And, when necessary, they realized when someone else in the store could better connect with a more timid or more bold shopper and handed off to another associate in the store, working as a seamless team.

Risk. Selling lingerie, especially risqué or, as the merchants in this chain called it, "glamorous" lingerie, is an edgy business. The high performers were more apt to ask questions that would make less lucky store managers blush, and did it with the style and finesse of a skilled medical professional or personal fitness coach. They invested more in building a relationship, not just looking for a sales transaction.

Will. Was the buoyant, upbeat, optimistic, can-do, confident attitude that the high performers projected a *cause* of their success, or was it a psychological by-product of their success? Honestly, we still don't know. What we do know is that it felt a whole lot better to be in the presence of these brilliant or lucky or high-courage store managers. Their enthusiasm was contagious. Service culture experts like Barry and Sasser have shown that shoppers can feel the difference in attitude that sets "service enthusiasts" apart from clerks or pushy salespeople — and reward that good feeling by being more open to their suggestions and spending more in their stores.

Fast forward to the post-utopian era

In every life sciences and healthcare investor conference, speaker after speaker tells us how tough the market has become. New discoveries have to be first-in-class, best-in-class or both. New therapies have to deliver breakthrough results in a way that is safe, error-free and user-friendly — and that makes payers say, "We need this new product on formulary, even if it costs more than the tools we gave caregivers yesterday." New IT solutions not only have to be upgrades on their own, they also have to integrate with existing systems — so the entire suite works smoothly, not just the specific breakthrough that you've innovated. What is Audacious and Aspirational earns a premium. What is easily and routinely Achievable is pedestrian, generic, "me-too," and is shopped until customers and payors get the best price they can, leaving the provider whatever meagre profit they can possibly eke out of the transaction.

At a recent BioMed Life Science Conference in Tel Aviv (2009), Orbimed's General Partner, Jonathan Silverstein, said that we are now living in the post-Utopian era. Investors will sit on the sidelines and wait until a concept has been proven and until the data say, "There's a clear line of sight to regulatory approval and adoption in the marketplace." There are fewer "get rich quick" opportunities, fewer diamonds in the rough that actually shine after all of the pressure it takes to get a product to be an asset with a good Return on Invested Capital (ROIC).

According to marketing guru Seth Godin (2012), healthcare and life sciences enterprises are not the only ones whose investors, payors and users demand better, faster, lighter, safer, higher-value solutions. Godin issued a stern warning to marketers about clever branding. Logos, colours, labels and slogans mean nothing unless teams on the frontlines and in the trenches are brilliant enough to deliver. Great inventions and poach-proof IP means little unless the value proposition cannot be replicated. A Credo or reputation is not enough; living up to your promise is what counts — with transparency and data to prove your claims are valid.

Some industries are victims of their own success. After each breakthrough, payors and users declare, "Nothing less will suffice," and set the bar higher. What was good enough before some clinics installed open MRIs and before Air Canada installed elegant business class seats called pods, is now punishment. Disasters also set the bar higher, when we investigate and declare, "Never again." What was good enough before the Fukushima meltdown, the Deepwater Horizon fire or the VIOXX recall is no longer an acceptable safety or regulatory standard.

As a result, even the most generous and encouraging executives cannot insulate their teams from stringent new requirements. They have to ask tougher questions. Accelerate timelines. Push the bounds of science, engineering, technology. And be courageous enough to challenge, probe, ask, critique, tweak — even if it makes some people uncomfortable. And they have to staff their Product Teams with leaders who can be sharp and eagle-eyed, and have the courage to find elusive opportunities.

Asking the impossible?

When Yael, the Chief Science Officer (CSO), entered the conference room that the lead project team had commandeered and asked about their preparations for next week's Ministry of Health review, she could feel their icy stares and resentment. The Project Manager winced. "This isn't a good time," he said.

Yael smiled and sat down anyway, apologizing and explaining that it was the only time she had. "Take me through your presentation," she said, "so I can see what you're putting together and reassure the board that we're on-track." Reluctantly, the team complied.

Within 10 minutes, Yael interrupted, voicing her displeasure with the group's work. "We need smart answers, not easy answers," she said, in a tone that sounded pleasant but was a clear reprimand for members of the team who overlooked problems that Yael caught without drilling down very far or breaking a sweat.

Yael's Project Manager rolled his eyes and groaned. This was exactly what he anticipated, having worked with Yael for years and knowing how hyper-critical and demanding she could be. "Here she goes again," he whispered to himself, quietly enough, he thought, not to be heard by anyone else. But others on the team heard his quiet protest and rolled their eyes, echoing their sympathy. Yael, they all knew, was an inveterate and unrepentant meddler who didn't know how to empower a good orchestrator to do his job. By the time the meeting ended, the tension was thick. Yael was fighting back tears and the team went from feeling "on top of their game" to wondering if they'd ever be able to meet Yael's standards, no matter how long and hard they worked.

Suppose you were a Project Manager with a demanding sponsor like Yael, who pushes you to take your Project Team beyond their collective comfort zones and insists on goals that are Audacious and Aggressive rather than what feels Achievable or Average? Where would *you* set the bar?

In the Utopian era, change leadership meant, "Slow down. Make it comfortable. Reel in luminaries who drink their own tonic, lest they get carried away, overreach and overcommit. Give lingerers a chance to catch up." And Luddites, the change-resisters and nay-sayers named after the 1890s protesters who burned down factories to preserve the livelihoods of the artisans who operated hand looms? Conventional change leadership said, "Give them a chance to complain and show them how you will address their concerns. Compromise to protect their interests." If you were operating in a traditional change leadership paradigm, you would look for a palatable compromise between Yael and the team – to preserve harmony and keep peace, rather than pushing for what's right.

In the post-Utopian era, we ask more of leaders. Like the high-performance Store Managers in the chain of lingerie stores, whose up-trending sales figures defied the downward pull of gravity, we expect Project Managers to:

Renew their Will. We expect them to rein in their frustration and perhaps, even their embarrassment when an advisor or a sponsor like Yael reminds them that something faster, better and more capital-efficient is needed. We expect them not to get "hooked." We expect them to cut through the tension, make a joke, lighten things up — not roll their eyes and fan the flames of indignation or resentment. We expect them to set the tone or change the tone for the team.

Refocus on Purpose. We expect them to recognize what's enterprise-critical and to create lift, when what's Audacious and Aggressive takes people to altitudes that make them acrophobic. We expect them not just to look in the rear-view mirror at the old trendline, but at the inflection points that will take success to new heights. We expect them to focus on what really adds value for end-users like patients and caregivers and their advocates like a Ministry of Health. If the Ministry of Health won't buy our story, as it is presented, and a sponsor like Yael says, "We have to do better, to attract the capital that will allow us to continue our work" we expect them to ask, "How can we make it happen?" rather than saying, "I just work here and report the data. What happens beyond that is not my job."

Open Candor. We expect them to pay attention to what's really important, not just bruised egos or encroached-upon turf. We expect them to raise tough issues and wrestle down enterprise-critical issues, or to help those who do. We expect them to notice when people are getting defensive because of personalities, gaffes or cultural differences that rub them the wrong way — and bridge those differences.

Refine Rigor. We expect them to anticipate the issues that need to be addressed to prepare for a key milestone, like a Ministry of Health review, and to mobilize the right people to weigh in on the right issues at the right time to ignite brilliance. We expect them to have collaborative designs, templates and roadmaps, probing questions and outside facilitators that can spark innovation. We expect them to help a stuck team to find the mystery shoppers and £50 notes, not keep turning the pages, fixated on BMW ads, on yesterday's customer profile or on a conventional unimaginative presentation to the Ministry of Health. If Yael walks into the room and asks a few questions that reveal unconventional, but promising, solutions, we expect uplifting courage-building Project Managers to say, "Eureka! Let's build a plan," rather than grousing, "Who needs all this extra work?"

Inspire Risk. We expect them to preserve the credibility and good name of other groups and to give colleagues the benefit of the doubt, rather than dividing the constituents into "them and us" rivalries. We expect them to intervene and remind colleagues, "Whoa, they are only trying to help; they're not the enemy!" and to restore trust. And to make sure that teammates feel appreciated, respected and fairly compensated, when they do pull together and create a success.

Step up, take charge and free your team from the shadow of leaders

Should Yael have been more encouraging with the members of the team who knew what she knew and saw what she saw? Yes. Should she have been more empowering and respectful of her Project Manager's authority? Also, yes. More proactive and timely with her feedback, so the group didn't have to pull together and upgrade their presentation with so little lead-time remaining? Less insulting and discouraging? No doubt.

But sponsors don't always remember what they've learned in management training classes or take the results of their 360-feedback assessments to heart. When they don't, who can blame the Project Manager in this all-too-real case for feeling discouraged? Who can blame him for losing Will, forgetting the Purpose, closing Candor, avoiding steps that should be built into their Rigor, and refusing to Risk. And for blaming Yael for being part of the problem, by casting a shadow that snuffs out brilliance and discourages the team.

Fortunately for everyone, Yael's Project Manager chose a different path. After a brief jolt, he shook off his indignation. He refused to be a victim. As the orchestrator of his team, he believed he had the power to set the tone, to use Yael's disapproval as a rallying point and call to action, to score a "win" for the enterprise with the Ministry of Health, even if they couldn't accomplish everything they first hoped they'd be able to get done. And Power Up the team's Brilliance.

As he sounded the call, the team responded. This wasn't because of some quick magic, but because he had established his leadership and his tone-setting role months before Yael swooped in and disrupted their harmony. It was because this wasn't the first time he said, "We can do better," and got them unstuck. It was because he was alert enough to look around the group, to listen to the clipped voices over the conference call and to read the terse emails, and see whose courage needed a boost with uplifting and ennobling. This wasn't the first time he approached Powering Up Brilliance like a physical therapist getting patients to exercise injured or atrophied muscles, knowing that they might need to be coaxed to stretch, and monitored to avoid permanent damage.

This also wasn't the first time the Project Manager told Yael, "I've got your back and can make you even more successful, if you give me the space I need to orchestrate the team." After a private conversation, Yael affirmed the Project Manager's authority and told him, publicly, "You're in charge." Was this the last time this drama played out? No. But it was another turning point, that built the team's resilience and ignited their own brilliance, even when Yael cast a darker shadow.

What's the lesson for you?

In training workshops, we run a strategy execution simulation. It's a hunt for medicinal herbs, where teams of 4-5 players race around the Haida Gwaii Islands, keeping their ships afloat and on course in storms and calm seas, high and low tides, shallows and deep water channels. The team that wins is the one that amasses the largest supply of material.

Some teams start at the beginning and work their way across the gameboard, one move at a time, from the start until they exhaust their resources. Their average scores are $120,500. Other teams start at the end and work backward to the beginning, before they leave the launchpoint and set out on their expedition. They amass a fortune that averages $350,000.

Both teams give themselves gold stars when you ask, "How did you perform?" It takes less than three minutes to do the arithmetic and figure out that far more than $350,000 is possible. But fewer than 20% of the teams think that way.

So, with this simulation in mind, we ask you, "What's possible?" Are you thinking backward, from the "A" level that's Aspirational or Audacious —

and seeing what you need to create an inflection point and achieve that success? Or do you settle for what's Average or Adequate, plodding forward, a step at a time, doing the best that you already know how to do?

Chapter 4
Conflict-Prone Realities in Conflict Averse Systems:
A Recipe for Fear, not Brilliance

To ignite brilliance and spur innovation, most enterprises have taken steps to break down silos and get people connected. They've tapped their luminaries to lead from the middle, and have put them in charge of bold initiatives, product upgrades, account teams or innovation task forces. They've used technology to increase connectivity and foster collaboration. Or they've redrawn the organization chart altogether, with matrix structures and centers of excellence bringing the right luminaries together to share brilliance and drive innovation.

All too often, the reality of complex networked structures and lead-from-the-middle assignments is very different from the promise. Rarely do they make people feel more empowered. The politics are fierce. Those who see promising opportunities — and want to seize them before they get away — find that the internal mobilization is even more daunting than the work they'll do externally with customers, investors, partners or regulators. Those who see safety, financial, quality or operational risks — and step up to lead — soon discover that many followers want to do their own thing and go their own way, rather than be told what to do. For anyone who tries to lead from the middle, it isn't easy to wrestle down tough issues and get your voice heard when you switch on your microphones and radio back to headquarters, "Houston (or Toronto, Paris, Shanghai or Tel Aviv), we have a problem" or "Wow. I've stumbled across a great opportunity!"

The complexities and challenges of navigating through networks, matrix structures and alliances — rather than hierarchies and chains of command — seem daunting for everyone, not just those in the middle. Even an all-powerful CEO, who was directed by his board to let go of the reins and rely on his middle managers to run enterprise-critical projects complained that the project teams and initiatives they set up eroded his power and made the organization less agile than it was when he cracked the whip and micro-managed everything himself.

In the face of more conflict, complexity, ambiguity and frustration, the obvious conclusion is that your organization is dysfunctional. That the culture is toxic. That moguls stifle innovation. That team dynamics are misunderstood or mismanaged. That people in power don't walk the talk of the values, credos or success behaviors they've put forward in their mission statement or posted on the website. That rather than cutting through red tape and bureaucracy, our approval mechanisms, budgeting processes and reward systems make it hard for luminaries to seize opportunities, challenge the status quo, flag or mitigate risks. That cross-functional teams, open systems and matrix structures simply don't live up to their hype.

Easy and obvious conclusions like these are true — *if* you bring conflict-averse expectations to systems and structures that are more conflict-prone than ever. Unless you know how to identify the landmines and defuse them, or when necessary, detonate them safely, it will feel like an act of self-sacrifice to push your initiative forward — rather than an act of courage. Unless you know how to decode team roles in a cross-functional team and how to mobilize support, it will look like chaos. Unless you know how the harmonies and rhythms should sound when boundaries are crossed and silos are merged, you'll be tempted to turn down the heat and slow the pace when something sounds like cacophony or syncopation.

This chapter will introduce you to a Head of Sales who answered the call when his Business Unit General Manager said, "We have to boost profits." He expected accolades when he found low-lying fruit and posted quick wins. But instead of getting everyone to sing from the same song-sheet, he found his innovation efforts stifled by landmines and moguls. Instead of igniting brilliance, he touched off a hailstorm of defensiveness and indignation. Instead of driving conflicts to a healthy resolution, he assumed they were noise, distractions, delays, resistance — and sought to discredit, isolate and neutralize his opposition and power through the obstacles. And was surprised when that only made things worse.

Fortunately, you can learn from this Head of Sales' missteps. You rein in your own frustration, impatience and indignation when some other departments react like lingerers or Luddites, rather than luminaries. You can embrace conflict prone realities rather than trying to neutralize or bypass the opposition. You can build the organization you want from the middle-out rather than waiting for it to be given to you from the top-down, recruiting partners to be part of your network and your virtual team. But first, let's meet Rami and take a look at the jam he created for himself.

How not to do it — after an auspicious start

The MD of a medical device company closed his office door and motioned for Rami to join him at the round conference table. He beamed. "As our new Head of Sales," the MD told Rami, "I'm expecting you to wean this organization off its addiction to discounts, promotions, special terms. We need to find ways to drive sales that don't dilute our profits. Customers tell us, over and over again, that our products are bulletproof and they'd never settle for a cheap substitute in their medical practices. So it doesn't make sense for us to give away the store and compete on price. This is your top priority. Let's see how quickly you can fix this problem."

It didn't take Rami long to analyze the figures, talk with his Regional Directors and see which "preferred" pricing schemes should be revamped. And to see which customers could benefit from extra services and product support, or could be stepped up into higher-value and higher-margin programs. In his past job Rami had an alliance with a leasing and financing company, that allowed customers to purchase higher-priced equipment without taking a hit on their cash flow. He talked with the same leasing company, and they were ready to offer the same terms to Rami's current customers — anytime he had a customer who was ready to sign the papers.

Rami sat down with the MD and presented his recommendations, less than a month after he was told to increase profits. The MD was wow'd. "How quickly can you execute these plans?" he asked, clearly endorsing Rami's proposals and giving him the green light to proceed. He didn't need to remind Rami that the CEO, Dr C, had said, "March or die," and expected them to look beyond business-as-usual, innovate and deliver quick results. When Rami replied that he could pull the switch and start the conversion in a matter of days, the MD got up and shook his hand. Rami beamed.

Fast forward four weeks. The Marketing Director of the medical device company and the Chief Counsel of the parent corporation ambushed Rami, calling an emergency Executive Team meeting to discuss Rami's pricing initiative. They presented a litany of complaints, miscalculations and indictments. It was an intervention, staged to get the MD to rein Rami in and put the brakes on his program, or demand that Rami resign. Rami was dumbfounded. And angry — because many of the worst accusations were direct quotes from his own Regional Directors, in complaints that should never been taken outside the chain of command in his own sales organization.

Rami was polite in the Executive Team meeting. He apologized for the misunderstanding and promised to "look into the problems." The MD, also blind-sided by the complaints, attempted to defuse the situation and encouraged everyone to get along and pull together to solve the problems. But as soon as Rami heard the accusations, he silently vowed that he would not tolerate blatant insubordination and disloyalty within his ranks. He already had a plan to reassign the Luddites in his team, dismantle their fiefdoms and neutralize their resistance and opposition. The "intervention" convinced him that he had to put that plan into motion — quickly.

In less than two weeks the opposition against Rami erupted into a firestorm. Rami was summoned to a full-fledged inquisition. The principal shareholder — who owned the holding company that owned Rami's medical device company — sat at the head of the conference room table, with the Chief Counsel seated to his right. The Marketing Head, who was Rami's worst critic, sat next to the Chief Counsel. They refused to speak or hear from Rami, and grilled the MD about "what he was doing, personally, to clean up the messes that Rami had created." Dr C, the CEO, who supported Rami's effort and who was instrumental in recruiting him into the company, was out of the country and his cellphone connection kept breaking up, leaving him unable to defend the MD or Rami against unbridled attacks or reassure the owner and his entourage that he would personally handle the problems.

Rami's critics came prepared. The Marketing Director unveiled graphs and trendlines, based on years of historical data, which showed how her preferred pricing, loyalty programs and bundled discounts were driving sales and should be preserved. The holding company's Finance Director entered the fray, with spreadsheets and illustrations showing that self-financing would be more profitable than the deal Rami hastily arranged with an outside bank, without her approval. The holding company's HR Director was also livid, siding with a lacklustre Regional Director whom Rami had demoted into a a scaled-down support role. The demoted Director was part of a protected class of employees and was threatening to sue the company for derailing his career, just because he told Rami the truth and criticized his pricing plan. Rami was incredulous. It was an ugly meeting.

When Rami was recruited for the Head of Sales job, he was warned that the executive team was dysfunctional. Dr C, the CEO, told Rami that the Chief Counsel and Head of Marketing had far too much access and sway with the owner of the holding company – and could subvert or kill ideas they didn't like. No one was immune from their naysaying, defensiveness and palace coup politics. Not even Dr C, let alone the MD. This wasn't a safe place for innovation. If veterans didn't like how their world was being rocked by an innovative idea that was "not invented here," all they had to do was appeal to the Chief Counsel. Within days, an edict would be issued — to put the innovation "on hold," until the owner himself could review the relevant facts with the CEO and decide whether the business benefit was enough to justify the discomfort, the investment and the risk.

The Chief Counsel truly believed the company needed her to be an advocate for loyal long-service managers whose job security and job satisfaction were being threatened by unproven ideas. Similarly, the Marketing Head saw herself as "defender of the loyal customers" whose interests could be threatened by reckless and ill-conceived schemes — which might earn a bonus for the MD and Head of Sales, but might erode the long-term value of the franchise. And the owner of the holding company appreciated their oversight and critical thinking — and prided himself on staying "close to the business" and providing a healthy creative tension in his interactions with his MDs. The CEO was growing more impatient and frustrated with the noise, and intercepted as many of these issues as possible — to give his division MDs the latitude to bring much-needed innovations to their businesses.

Was it messy? Definitely. Dysfunctional? Perhaps. But Rami didn't help to improve the situation, when he insisted that his position as Head of Sales should give him the latitude and discretion to pull the strings within his own chain of command, and get the support he needed to deliver "his" numbers. In fact, the more Rami insisted that it was enough to get the MD's approval, and they should respect his authority and defer to his judgment, the more his colleagues wanted him not just slowed down, but removed from his position altogether.

In his book, *Leading outside the Lines,* John Katzenbach (2010) warned that the informal organization — which connects business owners to long-service employees rather than MDs, customers to support functions rather than account executives, and co-workers to their friends and allies across the hall and across the ocean — has even more power to accelerate or block execution than the formal chain-of-command.   Richard Shell and Mario Moussa (2007), in *The Art of Woo,* advises leaders to map out a strategy to sell breakthrough ideas to their colleagues before charging forward.   Michael Watkins (2003) warns new leaders like Rami that their psychological contract and mandate are set within the first 90 days, and after that they reap the support they've sowed.

It's dysfunctional if a luminary, like Rami, doesn't stop, look and listen — long enough to read the interdependencies and forge the right alliances. Mistakes can be fatal to an initiative — and to the career of the person championing it — if he blows past flashing yellow lights, alienates power brokers and makes costly mistakes because he ignores criticism that slows him down or gets in his way. All that might have been anticipated and prevented by asking the right questions of the right people. And by stopping to listen and solve problems, before they limit your success. If only Rami had done that.

The orchestrator of an initiative, not the head of a silo
An array of stars and planets looks overwhelming and random for people who don't know how to read the night sky. They see chaos. They can't

decipher Orion's belt or the Southern Cross, let alone Leo the Lion or Pegasus the Flying Horse.

Similarly, leaders like Rami who are used to looking up and down a chain of command, and who define domains with boxes on the organization chart may not know how to map the white space in a matrix or informal network. If no straight lines or dotted lines appear on the formal organization chart, they may assume that none exist. If they are told to "march or die," they may assume that they don't have time to convene cross-functional task forces or consult colleagues in other departments or lower-level managers on the front lines.

A Harvard Business School study estimated that only 40% of all innovation programs — like this pricing initiative — are executed in a way that achieves the desired business impact (Kotter, 2012). Even when the strategy is correct, like it was for this medical device company, 60% of the initiatives either take too long and cost too much to deliver results — or fail to deliver enough innovation to make it worthwhile.

The studies are equally pessimistic about leaders who are hired, like Rami and his MD and CEO, to "shake things up" and upgrade key functions. Only 45% of the luminaries who set out to ignite brilliance are considered successes, one year after they are hired. Even when they have the experience and know-how and can see what needs to be done, all too often they fail to deliver the goods — or shake things up too hard and lose the trust of the troops they are leading.

When you talk with leaders like Rami who are crashing and burning, very few of them say, "Oops. Here are my mistakes. I need to lift my game and

73

do better." Instead, most of them talk about support that never materialized, about a lack of courage or brilliance on the part of those who recruited them, or dysfunctions in the team that failed to co-operate. They complain about being thrown under the bus by the informal, molecular networks and don't see the constellations, stepping stones and pathways that they could turn to their advantage, by stopping long enough to decode the labyrinth and work their way through the right touch-points.

Rami took his recruitment speech at face value. Who could blame him? It's seductive to believe a CEO like Dr C who inspires you with a "march-or-die" call to action. And to believe a MD who tells you that you were hired because you have the juice to turn things around, that you have his or her full support and that one single initiative is your number one priority. From a chain-of-command perspective, Rami assumed that his MD was the only sponsor who mattered — and the MD's approval and CEO's blessing gave him an express-track to push forward.

When luminaries like Rami see themselves as victims of Luddites who just don't "get it" and refuse to get out of the way, it's easy to dismiss dissent and risk assessments as resistance. "No wonder this company has such crummy margins, despite their best-in-class products," Rami said, shaking his head, to the consultant who'd been hired to help him get the pricing initiative back on track. "If the MD is serious about improving gross margins, he needs to tell the dinosaurs in marketing, legal, human resources, manufacturing and supply chain to stop second-guessing me and usurping my authority."

How You Define Your Ecosystem

SILOS & CHAINS OF COMMAND
Each function head issues orders and executes their part of the strategy

NETWORKS & MOLECULAR TEAMS
Multiple functions come together and sharpen each other's work

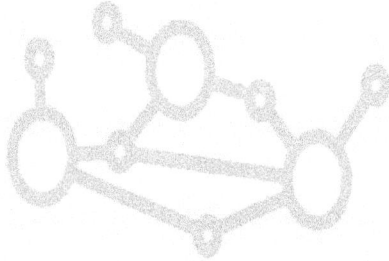

© 2012. www.courageinstitute.org • Tel: Israel: +972-3-7222754 • USA: +1-215-529-8918 • Canada: +1-819-300-6277

How You Define Your Place

BENEFICIARY, END-USER OR ADVOCATE
The customer, end-user, patient or buyer who is served by the enterprise

EXECUTOR
Step up to adhere to plans and make them happen as well as possible

ORCHESTRATOR
Reach out and mobilize the right players to do the right things in the right sequence

ADVISOR
Speak up to offer the best counsel and the best ideas

SPONSOR
Pay up or ante up with an investment of capital, bandwidth and reputation

© 2012. www.courageinstitute.org • Tel: Israel: +972-3-7222754 • USA: +1-215-529-8918 • Canada: +1-819-300-6277

Sometimes, of course, resistance is as destructive and dysfunctional as it seems. Some holdouts are more focused on preserving their power, prestige, entitlements and routines than contributing to innovation. Some are imposters who say the right things but fail to act. For a breakthrough to succeed, such holdouts need to be neutralized or moved out of the way. But more often than not, what looks like resistance or opposition is a conflict that needs to be embraced, to find the best solution rather than the easiest or fastest one.

Suppose Rami had approached pricing as a *enterprise-wide* initiative with enterprise-wide implications needing broad enterprise-wide participation — and not as a "sales issue" or as *"his"* opportunity to step up and outshine his colleagues. Suppose Rami had assumed that he had *multiple* sponsors and that his first priority was to bring them into alignment — with an Enterprise Project Management Office or Steering Team to mobilize, co-ordinate, woo and integrate joint efforts. Suppose he had seen himself as a leader who needed to ignite everyone's brilliance, not boss them around or outmaneuver them to win their acquiescence or compliance. This shift in perspective would have encouraged him to reach out differently to…

- A cautious Chief Counsel, who prided herself on risk-assessments to protect the holding company's owner and worried that 20+ year veterans and disgruntled customers could stir up trouble and involve the company in expensive litigation

- A well-connected board member, who took pride getting sweetheart deals for his favorite clinics and felt personally embarrassed by the company's new pricing policies and by Rami's insistence that they be applied across the board

- A Head of Marketing, who had served as interim Head of Sales and had lobbied unsuccessfully for Rami to report to her, and was an avid proponent of deep discounts to preferred customers and contracting with value-added resellers to provide after-sale support

- GMs of manufacturing plants, who used price concessions to appease customers put off by delivery delays, incomplete orders and shipping errors

- The CFO, who was just as concerned about inventory turns and aged receivables as he was about price realization and gross margins

- The owner of the parent corporation, who was annoyed that the controversy had reached him and that he was being asked to intervene while he was going through a messy divorce and didn't want publicity over higher prices to complicate his personal affairs.

"No one questions the fact that we have to make a better profit and that we have some opportunities that we've not yet seized," one of Rami's most vociferous critics said. "The question isn't whether or not we boost profits, it's *how* we do it intelligently and artfully — so we bring our customers with us. Rami forgets that we've all been in this business for quite a while and have learned a thing or two ourselves. If he had asked for our input, we could have prevented a lot of the problems that we're now scrambling to fix. That would have been a lot more productive than charging forward with a 'march or die' rallying call and getting defensive anytime someone said, 'Let's tread lightly.'" All we want is credit for being brilliant ourselves, rather than being treated like dummies or malingerers who don't have the best interests of the enterprise at heart.

What sets the stage for success?

More than 30 years of research tell us what conditions create fear and frustration — and stifle the brilliance of luminaries like Rami, who are eager to step up, show their stuff and make a difference. They also give us the antidote and tell us how to design jobs with a far higher motivational potential.

The easy and obvious implications of this research, which we reviewed in our first book, *The courage to act* (Klein & Napier, 2003), are simple and straightforward. Design jobs and parse out assignments to give luminaries like Rami clear priorities and give them room to run. Let them see the results as they go. Avoid conditions that create role ambiguity, role conflict, target creep and target blindness.

But the easy and obvious answers aren't necessarily the best ones. In a post-Utopian world that demands better faster leaner thinking to solve more complex problems in a hyperconnected and turbulent business environment, we have to learn to thrive under conditions like these — rather than crying, "Foul!" and declaring them "dysfunctional" when we run into these conflict-pone realities.

Role ambiguity. Leaders in the middle, like Rami, are more comfortable and secure when they know where they fit in, where career advancement can take them, what they have the authority to decide for themselves and where they need someone else's collaboration or approval. It doesn't seem fair to hold them accountable for decisions and outcomes, unless they also have control over the levers that have to be pulled, the resources that have to be deployed and the decisions that have to be taken to deliver the goods. To prevent unanticipated problems, we try to use frameworks like a RACI formula to clarify who has **R**esponsibility and **A**ccountability for team decisions (those in responsibility have a vote and those with accountability have veto-power) and to clarify which subject-matter experts to **C**onsult beforehand because of affected operations and to **I**nform them as well about final decisions. In a Utopian world, this all makes sense. But what if the problems that need to be solved are too complex for one single discipline (like sales) to have carte blanche and others (like marketing, HR, finance, supply chain, QA) to salute, respect their hegemony and follow their marching orders? What if multiple objectives have to be optimized, rather than trading off one success factor to maximize others? What if the opportunities that appear today will vanish in the time it takes for someone officially "in charge" to wake up, get up to speed, understand the complexities and ratify or overturn an on-the-fly decision? Or if risks have to be mitigated — now, not tomorrow — *before* we have to control the damages or recover from expensive mistakes? In this world, not only should we tolerate a level of role ambiguity — we should welcome and foster it, and use it to encourage anyone anywhere to step up and contribute their brilliance where and when it's needed to make a difference. Whether or not they have the authority.

Role conflict. If leaders in the middle, like Rami, are handed multiple goals, they would like those goals to be harmonized — lest we put them in "damned-if-you-do, damned-if-you-don't" double-binds and Catch-22s. They would like priorities defined by higher-ups, so saying, "Yes" to one set of priorities doesn't get them into trouble when they say, "No" or Not now" to something or someone else. If multiple sponsors have conflicting agendas or demand irreconcilably opposite success metrics, there's supposed to be someone at a higher level to intercede, adjudicate and insulate them from the wrath of those who feel that they've been let down. Conventional wisdom tells us to define metrics up-front and post them to provide a steady beacon, rather than changing every time there is a contravening opinion or an undercurrent of opposition.

Ask anyone who's accepted or forged a win/win agreement with opposing sides or political rivals and they'll tell you it requires more ingenuity and creativity than a compromise or winner-takes-all solution. The work isn't just intellectually demanding, but emotional as well. To look past threats and insults, positions and posturing. Listen for needs and for a solid logical business case. Rein in your frustration, impatience and indignation. Cut through or reduce the noise. Ask about what's possible, not just what's been done in the past or what's already tried-and-true. And, hardest of all, to presume good intentions and fiduciary responsibility, not gamespersonship and power plays — even when it's you who has to say, "Time out," and negotiate terms of engagement and a code of honor. If we're thinking of organizational hierarchies in a parent-to-child paradigm, of course we expect higher ups to do this heavy lifting for leaders in the middle like Rami and his antagonists. But if the structure is flat and matrixed, every orchestrator takes a turn as the lynchpin who holds everyone else on belay.

Target creep. If sponsors know their business, their operations and their competitive benchmarks, they're supposed to know what's feasible, what's aggressive and what's science fiction. They're supposed to intercede when customers, investors, partners or end-users demand the impossible. If an orchestrator like Rami is given a team that is ill-equipped, under-resourced, rushed, poorly trained and left out of the loop on vital information, who can blame them when mistakes occur, when quality is compromised or when progress stalls? That dysfunction is compounded, of course, when you speak up and assert your resource and information requirements — and are summarily dismissed and told to do the best you can with what you've already been given and are warned that failure is not a viable option, as Rami was told.

Yikes! Talk about blaming the victim! "I tried to tell Dr C and the MD that a pricing program like this takes a minimum of 18-24 months," Rami said, recalling a conversation that his sponsors had conveniently forgotten. In a business environment where C-level executives are pressed to deliver ever-better, ever-faster and ever-more-cost-efficient results, of course they're going to press luminaries like Rami and challenge them on timelines and resource constraints. They'll assume that every estimate of peak capacity has a safety margin before it revs up past the red line. They may probe, challenge, throw out ideas derived from articles they've read and days "when I used to do your job." They may not hear a gentle challenge like the one Rami remembers. If they're told, "This will be extremely difficult," they may not understand that the luminary really meant, "This could blow up in our faces and create even bigger problems."

If you see yourself as a subordinate who's "just following orders," you may feel vindicated if you can produce the emails you sent and the meeting notes that you recorded. But if you're a luminary who's accountable for getting your expertise heard and used, not just given and ignored, you'll be held to the expectations that you endorse by accepting an assignment — whether or not you thought those expectations were set at the right "A" level.

Target blindness. Naval ship commanders and fighter pilots understand that they have to focus on where the craft is sailing, not just the at what is in their gun-sights. Target blindness occurs when they shoot down the enemy but run aground or crash into the side of a mountain in the process, unaware of their context. That's exactly what happened to Rami. He was so fixated on price realization and on increased margins that he lost sight of the bigger issue — namely, his own standing with the teams he needed to mobilize and orchestrate. Like the ship commander who suddenly explains, "Oh, my Lord," as the craft takes a blow across its starboard bow, Rami was so focused on pricing victories that he was astonished to see how many of his colleagues he had alienated in the process. "Why didn't you tell me things were getting this bad?" he asked his MD.

Some orchestrators are better at reading the context than others. And some are better able to get feedback from subtle cues, rather than looking for affirmation and reassurance from their sponsors. Unfortunately, Rami wasn't one of them. Just as Rami was dumbfounded that the MD and Dr C hadn't picked up on his subtle protests about how quickly the pricing problem could be fixed, the MD was equally gobsmacked when Rami said no one had told him that his reputation was in trouble. "I wanted to be encouraging," the MD said, "so I balanced the criticisms I was hearing with praise for Rami's ingenuity and persistence." Rami assumed he was doing a good job and that his MD could live with the collateral damage. He had no idea it could be fatal.

Breaking free of the trendlines: The only way out is through

As we've described Rami's predicaments, we've referred to him as the orchestrator of the pricing initiative and have referred to executives like his MD, Dr C and the owner of the holding company as his Sponsors. This isn't just terminology. It's a change in perspective that equips middle managers to break out of hierarchy traps, where they look upward for permission and for edicts that imbue them with authority — rather than looking inward for the courage to step up, reach out and influence when they see what's possible and need more support to make it happen.

Orchestrators need to see past the "who reports to whom" boxes and lines on the chart — and see, instead, who is capable of making what contributions to the success of efforts like the pricing initiative — with themselves in the middle, integrating and facilitating the right movements between these players. For many middle managers like Rami, who are used to being "Head of This" or "Boss of That," thinking of themselves as Orchestrators is a Copernican revolution (Wind & Cook, 2006).

It means they need to assess the capabilities, political clout, bandwidth and motivations of the stakeholders they'd like to mobilize and bring into their gravitational field — and the orbits they'd like to mobilize each stakeholder to occupy as:

- **Sponsors who can approve and fund their initiative.** Rami assumed that the MD was the only Sponsor whom he needed to please – and that he had a "green light" when the MD, above him on the formal organization chart, said, "Looks good to the CEO and to me." He was wrong. The more your initiative has the potential to deliver breakthrough, disruptive results – and create an inflection point that breaks free of old trendlines and catapults the enterprise beyond incremental improvements – the more you'll need multiple Sponsors to "get it" and champion your efforts. Like, in Rami's case, the heads of other departments (like Marketing and Supply Chain), who saw how the pricing initiative, if successful, would make it harder for them to achieve their bonus objectives. And the principal shareholder of the holding company, who owned the medical device company and was asked to stake his franchise and family fortune on an out-of-the-box idea that had never been done before. Along with the owner's trusted advisors (like the Chief Counsel), to whom the owner turned and asked, "Honestly, is this *really* a good idea?"

- **Advisors who can bring new ideas and sharpen, refine, debug their thinking**. Perhaps, like Rami, you hear that others have expertise with innovations like those you are orchestrating. You may not immediately see their brilliance until they're asked for ideas, experiences and connections that can contribute to your success. Or are invited to weigh in, with risk assessments and risk mitigation. Rami wasn't

84

impressed with the first few ideas he heard. Whenever someone said, "Slow down. Danger ahead. Let's take a detour," he rolled his eyes and sighed, assuming they were too limited, risk-averse or turf-protective to "get it." As a result, he dismissed a lot of the brilliance that was available — and shut down debates that might have cost an hour or two of deliberation but saved weeks of damage control. "Rami acts like we're too stupid or naïve to optimize the company's profits," one of his critics said, "rather than understanding that we've all been down this road before and have made some progress. We've already made some of the same mistakes he's making and have experience that should be used so that we drive our re-pricing efforts without killing the franchise. All we want is for our expertise, experience and know-how to be used." Who could argue with that?

- **Executors who can get it done better, faster and cheaper.** Some of the resources you may need to deploy for "your" initiative could be housed within "your own" chain of command – and others may be housed in other silos, regions or business units. If so, not only do you need to add those "alien" or "foreign" resources to the planets orbiting as Executors; you also need to add the managers who allocate those resources as Sponsors. As you shift from decision-making to implementation, you may need some Advisors to fall into line and support team decisions, switching their orbit from Advisor to Executor, even if their ideas weren't adopted. And, if you deploy a Sponsor to make a presentation or push a delicate negotiation over the top, you, like Rami, might need to ask your MD, CEO or company owner to switch orbits and show up as an Executor who sticks to his/her marching orders rather than a Sponsor.

- **Co-orchestrators who lead other parallel initiatives.** With so many fast-track initiatives accelerating, so many people empowered to drive things forward and so much brilliance to ignite, so much darting in and out in crowded airspace, it's no wonder that there are a few harrowing moments, missed signals and even an occasional mid-air collision. In the world of hierarchies and chains-of-command, we expected higher-ups to keep track of all the initiatives in the portfolio and be mindful of saturation and capacity levels. If the system was overloaded, we pointed the finger upward — and waited until priorities could be clarified. In the world of flat teams and matrix structures, sponsors expect co-orchestrators to show up at portfolio meetings with the gaps mapped out — and, ideally, with recommended work-arounds, budget justifications, priorities and collaborative asset management. It's no longer enough for Rami — or you — to act like your initiative is the only or the primary innovation that's on the front burner.

- **Beneficiaries who buy, use and approve the products.** Ultimately, of course, Rami wasn't just asking constituents within his own company to stretch and work differently. He was also asking the users of the company's products to change their buying practices – and was asking the distributors to position and sell their products differently. He was also asking regulators to approve new claims and new therapeutic applications. No matter how much internal support he

86

mobilized and how well he overcame internal fear and reluctance, the success of the pricing initiative depended on caregivers, re-sellers and regulators embracing a different value proposition.

Suppose Rami had mapped his constituents. If so, he would have seen that there were more moving parts and interests than he first assumed when he defined the initiative as a "sales initiative" – both internally and externally.   He would see that some key stakeholders, like the Chief Counsel, would need to play multiple roles – as a Sponsor, an Advisor, Executor and advocate for Beneficiaries whom she knew better than anyone, because she had sat across the table with them and finalized their existing contracts. He would see that igniting brilliance required more than getting reluctant or fearful skeptics to say, "Yes," to his requests, but inviting them to sharpen up everyone's thinking, including his own, and share the wisdom of their previous attempts to command higher prices. He might have experienced a sense of loss, a feeling that his authority had been cut, that he was beholden to and dependent on factions who saw him as a rival. And a sense of confusion, since he was a newcomer who didn't know, for sure, who held the keys to what doors.

Because they create ambiguity, role conflict, target creep and target blindness, matrix structures, alliances, virtual and cross-functional teams are conflict-prone structures.   They can feel uncomfortable, when diverse perspectives create a dynamic, yin-and-yang creative tension. They can put you on the defensive, when some colleagues are, indeed, threatened and are preoccuped with defending their turf, protecting inflated budgets, justifying old routines and old trendlines. And create a chorus of cacophony and a tangle that's hard to unravel and navigate, as multiple sponsors weigh in with conflicting requirements and specifications and as multiple luminaries volunteer to be advisors.

At each of these inflection points, your courage — like Rami's — will be tested. Like Rami, you might look at the chaos and think, "This is dysfunctional." You might wish your CEO or MD had thought things through better and given you more power and authority, so you can "make" people show up on time, give you the input you want and, when it's time to push forward, adhere to your directions. It will be tempting to indulge your reptilian or mammalian instincts and fight-or-flight — rather than switching on the sgACC in your cerebral cortex to be a fearful (or insulted) *non*-retreater and Power Up Brilliance. Here's a response we heard from one C-suite executive, when these concerns were voiced by middle managers like Rami who were being prepared to Power Up Brilliance from the middle-out:

"In our old chain-of-command, you could play 'good child' and be absolved of responsibility, as long as you followed orders and delegated tough decisions upward. Our matrix structure asks us all to step up like adults and take charge of deliberations in an adult-to-adult, rather than child-to- parent, way. Yes, it was a lot more comfortable being a child than being an adult. But, if we embrace our role as orchesrators, we can have a lot more fun. Influence. And opportunity to really make a difference. For the business. And for the patients and caregivers who should be using our medical devices properly. As senior executives, we have to be more effective as sponsors, just as you need to be better at orchestrating. We are all learning to lift our game. Together."

In one short statement, this C-level executive challenged orchestrators to embrace the mantle of courage and exhibit all 5 Activators:

- **Rigor** — to place themselves in the center of the moving parts, as the orchestrator, and to map the partners they'd need to mobilize, wherever they reside on the formal organization chart
- **Candor** — to take charge of deliberations, make sure that the right issues are put "on the table" and are pressure-tested to put forward the best solutions, not necessarily the easy or obvious ones
- **Risk** — to approach conflict-prone realities with an adult-to-adult perspective and the trust that everyone wants what's best for enterprise success
- **Purpose** — to set everyone's sights on making a difference for patients and caregivers, the users and beneficiaries of the company's products, even when that stretches lingerers and Luddites out of their comfort zones and beyond the security of familiar tried-and-true trendlines
- **Will** — to stretch, lift their game, take pride in their gains and renew each other's energy, together.

Isn't this a lot of extra work?

Yes. And a lot of hand-holding, ego-stroking, listening, reassuring and relationship-building. Rami isn't the first take-charge, no-nonsense, "I've-got-a-job-to-do" technical leader who's rolled his eyes when we've described the steps needed to Power Up Brilliance in a frightened and entrenched team. And who's said, "Get out of my way. Don't tell me about reaching out and mobilizing a network. You're slowing me down."

Even in a network that is simpler, where everyone reports to you in a straight chain of command, chances are that you need more than a collection of executors, waiting for you to give direction, crack the whip and do as you tell them to do. You need thinkers, problem-solvers, opportunity-spotters, initiative-takers. You need entreprenuers who are more focused on what external beneficiaries want and need than on "what will please the boss." You need presenters who put their own style, panache, authenticity into the scripts and powerpoint decks they're given. Rami needed finesse, not just a spreadsheet, to raise prices and wean his community off of deep discounts and special concessions. And, yes, that's a lot of extra work.

Chapter 5
Dare to Stand Out:
Overcome the Bias Against Creativity

It doesn't take long for creative idea-generators to see that their brilliance get them into trouble. Even when leaders set the bar high and say they want breakthrough thinking, that doesn't mean they are comfortable with creative personalities or that they enjoy the creative process.

According to research at Cornell's School of Labor and Industrial Relations, reported by Jennifer Mueller and her associates (2011), there's a bias against creative people. Given a choice, most of us prefer to work with colleagues who make us feel secure rather than those who shake things up. We like steady-as-she-goes predictability, not serendipity or surprises. We might be entertained by colleagues who think out-of-the-box or who flaunt their idiosyncrasies, but we are apt to blow off their breakthrough ideas as "too radical" and "too out of touch with reality." We get impatient when creative people ask probing generative questions and scratch their chins rather than saying, "We're good to go. Full speed ahead."

In the face of the bias against creativity, it's no wonder that brilliant standouts are afraid to say, "I've got a better idea," or, "Let's talk about the elephant in the room." It's no wonder that they hold back, even when they're exhorted to stand up and speak out by Corporate Values and Success Behaviors that are written in company handbooks, in credos and in plaques that hang on the wall of meeting rooms. One brilliant innovator told us, "Putting forward an original idea in this company is like being a duck in an arcade. They tell us we should 'be brave' and 'learn from everyone,' and that we should 'get the elephants on the table.' But that doesn't mean they'll cheer for us when we step up and give them a big breakthrough Idea. You need a tough skin, a bulldozer's power and a loud voice to get heard in this crowd."

Intellectually, we know what happens when we stifle brilliance. Groupthink. Premature consensus. Peer pressure. Teammates who follow orders, rather than taking initiative and charting a better course of action. Teammates who keep their heads below the parapets and become bystanders, rather than protagonists, when they aren't sure whether their ideas — and their very presence — will get a receptive welcome (Gerstein and Shaw, 2009). Who collude with what author Rod Napier (2013) calls "seduction of the leader," rather than challenging those who can make or break their careers and their reputations, or influence this year's pay raise or performance bonus.

Jerry Harvey (1988) referred to this "go-along-to-get-along" dynamic as "the Abilene paradox." We end up in Abilene when smart people who know we should be in Dallas or Tokyo keep quiet about the real opportunities and go along for the ride to a less promising destination (i.e., Abilene). It takes courage, Harvey noted, to step forward, speak up and become what he called a constructive confronter; i.e., "to own up to your conclusions, put them forward and be open to the feedback and challenges that you may get" when you lift your voice and say what is obvious to you, knowing that a contrary viewpoint or an original non-conventional out-of-the-box idea might not be what some members of your group want to hear.

In nearly every enterprise, some groups are higher on the innovation hierarchy than others. If you are high-up on this thought-leadership hierarchy, you have the mandate to be a "constructive confronter." To say, "Wait, let's probe deeper." To dream up new possibilities and formulate new strategies. If you are part of the innovation elite, you may not encounter much of the bias against creativity. You can be a bulldozer, when there is a higher Purpose to achieve. But if you are lower on the innovation hierarchy – in a discipline that has been a support function rather than a source of innovation (like IT or Project Management, Safety or Finance), or in a one-down age group or an ethnic minority – you are more likely to be dismissed or ridiculed. Heck, you may not even get permission to speak when you clear your throat and try to talk.

Deepwater Horizon, the BP off-shore oil rig that exploded, polluting the Gulf of Mexico. Enron. British Leyland's QA and design problems, using Lucas electrical components (the prince of darkness). Bhopal's chemical spill. Vioxx. The explosions that killed everyone aboard the Columbia and Challenger space shuttles. The demise of RIM and Microsoft's battle back to regain market share, after Apple and Google out-innovated them and introduced refined versions of products that they had rejected as too "out there." Kodak dismissing digital photography as a passing fad that didn't fit into their core business, until it was too little too late. All of these missed opportunities have one thing in common. They were foreseen by luminaries who stood up and said, "Just a minute," and were ridiculed for their brilliance. Who can blame them for keeping their heads below the parapets, rather than stepping up as "constructive confronters?" Who can blame them, when they faced icy stares or sharp rebukes, for second-guessing their own judgment, only to find out too late that they were, in fact, right all along?

In this chapter, we'll describe a business transformation that asked luminaries low on the innovation hierarchy to step up as "constructive confronters." As soon as they did, they ran into the bias against creativity. But they learned to approach the adversity with courage. So can you, when your enterprise asks you for a high level of brilliance but then makes it hard to get your creativity and probing insights used. With the the skill to lift…

- **Your own Will** — when you see your political standing, popularity or, possibly your livelihood, flash in front of your eyes and are afraid of the consequences of letting your brilliance shine
- **Risk** — by taking the time to build trust and credibility and confront in a way that says, "I'm on your side" and "I've got your back," rather than, "I'm part of the opposition."
- **Lift Purpose** — to a level that gets everyone to see what's possible and that achieves multiple objectives rather than trade-offs; e.g., profit *and* market share, safety *and* cost-effectiveness, customer loyalty *and* employee engagement
- **Adopt Rigor** — so you are seen as "part of the solution" rather than "part of the problem"
- **Open Candor** — for a foundation of support so you are not alone when you step up and speak out as a "constructive confronter"

Dare to invert the hegemony hierarchy

EBI was a specialty insurance company that outperformed its industry by a 33% margin. Lots of competitors tried to replicate their success formula, but couldn't build a culture that Powered Up Brilliance as well as EBI did.

EBI's success formula started with a simple discovery. By law, insurance rates were set based on a policyholder's safety record. Employers with high accident rates pay a higher premium than those who file fewer claims. Their CEO looked at this tried-and-true formula and asked, "What if we could dramatically improve a policyholder's safety performance — quickly?" The answer was clear. EBI could charge policyholders based on their old accident rates, and could pay claims based on the new safety record. On paper, it was a business model that was far more profitable than insuring even the best accident risks — if they could actually improve a policyholder's safety record.

That's where Donny came in. He was a 35-year-old Loss Control engineer, working in a region that was 3000 km (1800 miles) and a world away from the Corporate HQ. He was jazzed by the "zero accidents" strategy — and bored by the old Loss Control job, inspecting workplaces, analyzing spreadsheets, filing reports. Years of service as a Safety Officer in the Navy give Donny the smarts to ask the right questions, in English and Spanish, and the operational savvy to understand the implications of safety improvements that affect productivity and capital upgrades. Donny was 10 years out of the service, but still had a trim physique, a bounce in his step and a smile on his face. He was ready and eager to step up, speak out and guide his team — to show them how to bring Zero Accidents to life.

An account manager, dressed in an expensive suit, leaned across the table, stared over his bifocals and with patronizing faux patience, told Donny, "I know someone from your side of the tracks never actually ran a business or had to make tough decisions about where to spend money in facility upgrades." His voice was soft but the message was clear. Back off. Slow down. Know your place. Be subordinate. Yield to higher-paid teammates in roles that have always had more power and hegemony and are used to calling the shots and making the tough calls.

In nearly every industry, there is an innovation hierarchy. Those at the top have the hegemony, clout, mandate to put forward bold new proposals. They seem exempt from the bias against creativity. But those in support roles, like Donny, are dismissed as uppity, obstructionist, uncooperative when they say, "Here's something new," even when they are right and even when they support the company's espoused business strategy.

It was the typical Catch-22. EBI's executives, especially the CEO, said they wanted Loss Control leaders like Donny to show up with brilliance, to think out of the box, to propose improvements that would prevent accidents, injuries and fatalities in the workplace. But when Donny spoke up and said, "Here are the risks we need to mitigate and here's how to get it done," he ran into the brick wall that our friends from Cornell describe as the bias against creativity.

At that moment of truth, Donny had the power to decide whether EBI's Zero Accidents strategy was for real — or not. It was all in his hands. EBI's CEO wasn't in the room when this policyholder's account was debated and the underwriting recommendations were put forward. Donny alone had the power to decide whether to be a "constructive confronter," or whether to avoid the controversy and give the account manager a package that would be easier to sell. Donny needed courage to stare down the veiled threats and incendiary remarks.

Ask Donny about what it took to stand firm and he'll smile and quote the American actor, John Wayne, saying, "Courage is being scared to death — and saddling up anyway." Remember what we said in Chapter 2 about being a fearful non-retreater? On days when he knew he'd face skeptical and non-receptive Luddites and laggards waiting to see which way the wind would blow, Donny could feel his heart pound and his mouth get dry when he entered the meeting room. His wife and friends knew it would be a tough day and wished him well. The mini-insults and assaults on his professionalism and ethnicity did not go over his head; he simply refused to be goaded into a fight that would be on someone else's terms and would take the discussion where he didn't want it to go.

Donny might follow Wayne's quote with this Spanish proverb: *"Lo cortés no quita lo valiente* (Courtesy does not exclude courage.)" To recognize that courage doesn't have to roar, but can speak softly and politely, as long as it doesn't back down or go silent. With:

- **Purpose** — to keep his eye on the prize; i.e., the "zero accidents workplace" that EBI was selling to accident-prone employers
- **Will** — to show up as an equal, maintaining a sense of humor and composure, exuding confidence, even when taunted or belittled, and to take joy in winning over skeptics and wrestling down key issues and sharing the joy you feel

- **Candor** — to handle bullying with finesse, lest he say or do something that would further antagonize his detractors and compromise his credibility

- **Rigor** — to anticipate the concerns that policyholders and account managers would raise about safety upgrades and come prepared to show them a viable plan, with a strong business case

- **Risk** — to engender the trust that would allow an account manager and underwriter to put their success — and the fate of their enterprise — in Donny's hands, knowing (as they all did) that the policyholder would balk at Donny's recommendations

EBI's success formula wasn't hard to understand. It was as simple as "buy low, sell high." Start with a customer who has a poor safety record and has to pay a high fee to insure its workers. Reduce accidents, so there are fewer claims to cover. Pocket the profits. So why couldn't other insurance companies replicate EBI's success, when they tried to copy its success formula?

The answer is simple. They didn't build enough courage to Power Up Brilliance. As a result, in other companies, Loss Prevention Engineers caved when they faced moments of truth like Donny's and faced the bias against creativity. Rather than looking fear, politics, taunts in the face and lifting others above these limiters, they gave in to power-down dynamics. They were co-operative, acquiescent, supportive team players. But they didn't move the needle on safety in the way that Donny mobilized his account teams to do.

Dare to see past a "victim perspective"

Having an MD, PhD or Professor-level credential doesn't insulate thought-leaders from the bias against creativity, if they have a low position on the innovation hierarchy. In the half-life of business cases, the Vioxx recall is ancient history. But it's had a lasting, perhaps permanent, impact on the standards that drug companies have to meet to bring a new drug to the market. Regulatory agencies scrutinize a drug company's dossier more aggressively and look for reasons to deny, rather than approve, their applications. As a result, MDs and PhDs who understand safety, regulatory requirements and product liability have been asked to step up, reach out, dig deeper and innovate more boldly than ever before.

Amita was a luminary drug safety director, recruited by a global pharmaceutical company for a key role with a promising asset that, despite its strong therapeutic benefits, had a tricky safety profile. "How," the product team asked, "do we mitigate the risks, so physicians know when this particular drug therapy is contraindicated — and so they respond quickly if (G-d forbid) there is an adverse reaction to the drug?"

Despite the fact that Amita's expertise was needed, she faced the bias against creativity when she asked "elephant-in-the-room" questions, pinpointed the risks that any vigilant regulatory agency would identify, and proposed risk mitigation measures. As a woman, an Indian immigrant and a safety expert standing her ground with gung-ho clinical researchers and product champions, she developed a thick skin. But that thick skin didn't keep her from resenting the obvious scorn that she routinely endured. "As soon as I walk into a room, the conversation ends. People avoid eye contact. They snicker when I present my findings. Or they cut me off and talk over me. I feel like a pariah and I don't see anyone else having to work this hard to overcome such skepticism and negativity."

Amita's moments of truth were not that different from Donny's at EBI. And she thought she was responding to them with courage. But her breed of courage was a deadly combination of righteous indignation (in private) and stonewall intransigence (in public).

Amita told us that the problem wasn't one that she had created. "If they would give me the respect they did when they recruited me for this position," she told us bluntly, "we would be far more creative. We would get past the gridlock and would put forward some brilliant new ideas about how to treat this awful disease." Of course, Amita was right. But the way she responded to the bias against creativity made her ineffective as a constructive confronter. That made her part of the problem, stuck at a lower-than-needed level on the innovation hierarchy.

Amita approached the bias against creativity with an external locus of control. She wasn't aware that she was giving away her power. But the more she defined the problem as "how they are treating me," and insisted that we should be coaching her antagonists to "be more open-minded and generative," the more stuck she became. We felt her pain. It's never fun to be in a one-down position, chastised for the very insights and ideas you are responsible for bringing forward.

More than a half-century ago, Julian Rotter (1954) showed that people who face the bias against creativity with an internal locus of control are far more effective at earning the support they crave. Instead of saying, "This is not my fault" (which, often, is true), they ask, "How can I turn things around?" and "Whom can I mobilize to help?" To:

- **Fulfill Purpose** — to stay focused on what really matters (namely, getting the drug approved, with a safety profile that would prevent product liability suits) and remind distracted colleagues what is more important than turf and hegemony

- **Renew Will** — to keep your energy high, your alertness sharp, your confidence up, and to take the issues seriously without taking yourself too seriously

- **Entrust for Risk** — to look past turf struggles, defuse we/they battle-lines, and cry "foul," when necessary, in a way that insists on the respect and credibility you deserve (rather than complaining about the respect you aren't yet commanding)

- **Open Candor** — so facts and logic guide deliberations more than biases, and so "what if" scenarios can chart new trendlines and create inflection points

- **Strengthen Rigor** — to look beyond winning and losing the debate, and use everyone's creative energy, skeptics and critics included, to sharpen up proposals, wrestle down and mitigate risks, pressure-test plans and leave room for improvisation and serendipity.

Can anyone dare to step up?

In North America, D.A.R.E. is an anagram accompanied by the slogan, "Just say, 'No.'" The letters abbreviate the name, Drug Abuse Resistance

Education. With the right level of courage, they claim, young people can resist peer pressure and keep themselves sober, even if others are taking a chemically induced trip to Abilene.

Ask anyone who's taken D.A.R.E.'s message to heart and they'll tell you there are prices to pay, when you keep your eye on the prize of a healthy, possibility-filled drug-free life. There are childhood friends you have to leave behind. There are parties you don't get invited to anymore, even as a designated driver. Sometimes the shunning is quiet, even benign. They just leave you alone. And sometimes it gets ugly, even threatening. D.A.R.E. builds the courage that kids need to sustain pride and a sense of accomplishment, and to delay gratification in pursuit of a bigger life "win." With the D.A.R.E. formula, they'll tell you, anyone can learn that courage.

In a democratic, egalitarian society, we believe that everyone is capable of making a contribution. We believe there's social justice in the "one person, one vote" formula — and that decisions are better shaped through consensus and compromise rather than fiat and autocratic decree. But there's more to this social contract than rights and privileges. There's also responsibility. That's why Infinity Pharmaceuticals CEO Steven Holzman expected key thought-leaders to be mindful of the business, ethical and medical consequences of their decisions, with a perspective that he called "citizen ownership."

In his 2007 book, *Assault on reason,* Former US Vice President Al Gore warned that democracy can be hijacked unless we are educated and sophisticated enough to make good decisions. As citizens of a republic or of an enterprise, Gore said, we have an obligation to educate ourselves about the facts and the data, and make scientifically valid predictions about the consequences of our actions and decisions. Without reason — and the heavy lifting it takes to make competent, not just ideological, decisions — Gore warned that we can become prey to a new form of tyranny.

The same is true in business. All too often, we hear project teams (or, even worse, executive teams) politicize deliberations with comments like, "Ignore them. They do not believe in HR," rather than embracing the criticism and challenge of finance experts who ask about the ROI. We hear customer advocates propose expensive give-aways that, while nice, have no real impact on loyalty or net promoter scores. We hear pragmatic COOs trivialize engagement survey results and refuse to see how it affects market share and profits, dismissing data with a wave of their hands.

Sadly, not every corporate citizen has the same level of astuteness, foresight or peripheral vision. Not everyone grasps the complexities. Not every Pharmacovigilance professional can start with a clean sheet of paper and design a risk-mitigation program from the ground-up, knowing what is medically and financially sound as well as what will protect patient safety. Not every supply chain professional has enough grasp of the interdependencies to be more than a replenishment administrator. Not every Project Manager can look forward to see what will accelerate a program and produce better products, rather than looking backward at milestones and budgets that have (and have not) been achieved.

The courage to create an inflection point isn't just about stepping up. It's also knowing when to step back and be open to perspectives that are ideologically threatening, but empirically sound. It's knowing what you don't know and how to tap other experts, get them to step up, and rely on someone else's judgment.

EBI's success was produced by a cadre of Loss Prevention Engineers like Donny, who refused to surrender to the bias against creativity. It was equally produced by account managers and underwriters, who owned up to their ideological preconceptions and embraced a new way of thinking about insurance — as a vehicle to promote socially responsible management and show that worker safety isn't just good manners, but is also good business.

If you are at the top of the innovation hierarchy, like EBI's account managers or Amita's Medical Directors and product champions, it takes courage to:

- **Risk** — and rely on the data, business cases and inflection points put forward by thought-leaders who see things differently from you. If you are Rami (the Head of Sales with the controversial pricing initiative profiled in Chapter 4), it is a risk to listen to Marketing and Legal professionals and go slow at the beginning to go fast later, and to put your success in their hands.

- **Open Candor** — and make data-driven, reasoned, empirically-sound decisions rather than ideological ones, and to ask tough questions about business cases that rely on reasoning that says, "We invest and work and invest, and then we have a miracle and the results magically happen."

- **Practice Rigor** — when it seems easier and faster to take decisions unilaterally or to pack the room with people who will agree with your ideology and will not insist on a bullet-proof plan of action.

- **Renew your Will** — when you are asked to cede power, share hegemony or when you personally are becoming threatened or impatient with the process

- **Stay focused on Purpose** — rather than allowing yourself to get distracted by politics, lulled into a false sense of security, or seduced into compromising rather than optimizing your profits and your opportunity to make a meaningful difference.

How you hire for your enterprise or project team makes a big impact on whether you have teammates who are capable of looking past ideology or short-sightedness, and giving you the thought-leadership you need. That's why Dynamix Pharmaceuticals CEO Dr Oren Becker hires large. Becker wants experts who can look deep and broad — and acknowledges that it's easier to find one or the other, but not both. In Hebrew, he calls the perspective that he wants a *rosh gadol* (or large head) — with the emotional intelligence and maturity to welcome a robust debate, that generates new possibilities and breakthrough ideas rather than deteriorating into a game of wits about who's right and who's wrong. Can anyone fit into the culture that Becker is building at Dynamix? He'll tell you that the answer is, "No."

Do some cultures encourage daring more than others?

Dutch psychologist Geert Hoffstede (2010) devoted his career to the study of cultural differences among diverse nationalities. Hoffstede identified a number of markers that describe unique styles of "deep thinking" that are encoded into the national psyche of Americans, Brits, Canadians, Germans,

French, Israelis and virtually every nationality at a young age.

One of Hoffstede's markers is what he termed "power-distance." In high power-distance cultures, "the less powerful members of society expect and accept that power is distributed unequally." What are the implications of that acceptance? In high power-distance cultures, people are highly attuned to where they reside in a pecking order or innovation hierarchy. When they enter a new team, they quickly figure out who's above them and who's below them in hegemony, whether or not that's reflected in job titles and Hay points. Once they know where they stand, they adhere to the limits of that pecking order. In deliberations, they defer to those above them, withholding ideas or questions that could embarrass or "show up" their superiors. Those at higher levels have responsibility, not just privilege. They show the noblesse oblige to support those below them with clearly defined bounds of authority and with clear marching orders.

The criteria that define high-status and low-status might differ from one power-distance society to another. In Japan and France, where you sit on the organization chart grants or denies you Elite status. So does your ability to speak the language perfectly, without any trace of a foreign accent or regional dialect. In Germany, the hierarchy is based on academic credentials, with those at Professor status expecting a level of reverence and obedience that technicians cannot command. In other societies, the hierarchy is based on wealth and capital, social caste, race or ethnicity, gender or age. If you are in a high or moderate power-distant culture, you are more likely to be a victim of the bias against creativity if you step up, speak up, reach out and overreach your station. And will need an extra measure of creativity, initiative and innovation — not just to see a promising opportunity or a breakthrough solution, but to get someone of a higher status to be your spokesperson, your advocate or your connector.

Israel has one of the world's lowest power-distance scores, even in its Army. No wonder it's more prevalent to find a more robust and generative debate in Israeli ventures than in many other national cultures. Denmark and Holland are also known for low power-distance scores. No wonder their middle managers and technical experts are also known for asking blunt, direct questions of their superiors and pointing out mistakes and miscalculations quickly, without worry that their criticisms could be off-putting or could evoke any fear of retribution or accusation of insubordination.

On the surface, this sounds ideal and almost utopian. No one to stifle your Candor when you lift your voice or to thwart your Will when you step up with enthusiasm and say, "Eureka! Here's a terrific idea." As long as we're aligned on Purpose, co-ordinate with Rigor and Risk enough to trust and support other parts of the team, a flat Power-Distance culture should be a great climate for innovation.

But if you think that the openness of a flat Power-Distance culture takes less courage, think again. Ask any American executive what it's like to lead a team of Israelis and they'll likely echo the sentiments that we heard expressed by Todd Wallach, the American who'd been recruited to take the reins as CEO of Molecular Detection. "The first time I met with our Israeli leadership team," Wallach says with a wry smile, "my first instinct was to fire them all for blatant disrespect or to assert my authority and show them who's the boss. What chutzpah to challenge the new CEO on his first visit to Israel and demand an explanation of why capital investments are being allocated in a particular way and to tell me how I could do my job better. But then I listened. And, the fact is, they asked very intelligent questions and understood the balance sheets, the nuances, the business and the strategic implications quite well. It wasn't a power play or a coup d'etat at all; it was doing their part to help all of us, and to support me doing the very best job I could as their new CEO."

In our first meeting, Dr William Polvino, the CEO of Veloxis, an American-Danish company, shared a similar observation with us. Like Israel, Denmark is a low Power-Distance culture. This CEO "got it," much like Wallach. "I love working with the Danes," he told us. "They're blunt. If they think you're wrong, they tell you in a direct straightforward way. There's no meeting after the meeting needed to ponder the nuances and wonder what they really meant to say. They assume you're an adult, a professional, that you've got your emotions in check and your ego under control. Problem is, some of the Americans in our team don't have the courage to listen and fall back into debates about who owns what turf and who has the authority to get their judgment to prevail."

Inverting the innovation hierarchy, as Polvino and Wallach point out, takes courage from the top-down and middle-out, not just from the bottom-up. If you've been at the top of the hierarchy and now find the hierarchy inverted or flattened, you'll need...

- **Candor** to listen without prejudice or "kill-the-messenger" dismissiveness
- **Risk** to share power and rely on someone else's expertise

- **Rigor** to rely on data, logic and projections rather than turf or authority
- **Purpose** to stay focused on enterprise-success not parochial hegemony
- **Will** to make it fun and joyful to sharpen up each other's thinking

If you've been at the bottom of the hierarchy, and have promising ideas, enterprise-critical insights or breakthrough foresight, you'll need courage to step up to the front of the bus and invert the hierarchy. You'll need...

- **Purpose** to assess, "Why?" and "Why now?" with business acumen
- **Candor** to put forward your ideas in a way that they can get heard
- **Rigor** to make your case and to map the stepping stones to get heard
- **Risk** to assume good intentions even in the face of vigorous opposition
- **Will** to sustain and renew your enthusiasm, despite opposition or inertia

And those in the middle of an innovation hierarchy? If you're a CEO like Todd Wallach, Bill Polvino or Oren Becker, you may see the stand-off between those who've been at the top of the innovation or thought-leadership hierarchy and those who've traditionally been at the bottom. You may be a cross-cultural bystander who sees the tension between those in a lower Power-Distance culture and those in a moderate or high Power-Distance culture. Or you may be Project Leaders or Account Team Leaders, orchestrating the efforts of a cross-functional and multi-cultural team. From the middle-out, you'll need ...

- **Purpose** to define "what success looks like" and to establish criteria to optimize enterprise-success
- **Risk** with a code of honor to bring factions together and expect them to transcend turf issues or political rivalries
- **Rigor** to design a process that will lead to a productive debate and decisions made on business cases and data rather than ideology
- **Candor** to use diverse perspectives and new insights to go wild, spark generative discussions and power innovation
- **Will** to infuse an optimistic spirit and infectious enthusiasm into the team and to make sure that tension is met with joy and enthusiasm rather than fear and frustration

Chapter 6
Who's Running Your Deal?
Boost Yourself Out of Hierarchy Traps

Something special is encoded into the way we manage up. It starts at a very early age. We can see it in our infant grandson, Itzi. Before he could utter a word, he could recognize each of his parents — and knew which of them was best at what. He "got it" by smell, taste and feel, as well as by sight and sound. Sitting with the entire extended family at Passover, we could see that he'd taken charge of a complex matrix, before age two, and had put each parent, grandparent, step-grandparent, aunt, uncle and great-grandparent on a separate and distinct training program. We each had our special words and songs, games and routines, and all he had to do was wind each of us up and hit the "play" button.

It's fun to watch Itzi, be part of his entourage and to have our own special one-to-one routines. But his mastery of the matrix doesn't make him exceptional. All of the young toddlers in his *gan* "get it." Before age two, they recognize parents and teachers, grandparents and doctors, aunts and uncles, caregivers and rabbis. They know who's who — and understand which relationships are peripheral, and which really are "high-stakes." They each have their own routines to manage up — to reach out, woo higher-ups and get them to do what they want them to do, now. And they keep refining their manage-up techniques, until they find what works with whom.

111

In his book, *Outliers: The story of success,* Malcolm Gladwell (2008) described two gifted mathematicians — one, a top-flight genius, whose career derailed because of a minor technicality and the other, a bit less gifted technically, whose career took off even though he needed special dispensation to meet the entrance requirements. The key difference, Gladwell noted, is that the successful mathematician knew how to manage up. Like our grandson, Itzi, and most of Itzi's classmates, he knew how to charm those in authority — so they would bend the rules and open opportunities to him. The one who derailed, on the other hand, flaunted his genius and superiority — and alienated higher-ups who were in a position to help (or not help).

Deferring is not the answer

This was Sarit's lucky break. She earned it. Like the high-performing mathematician cited by Malcolm Gladwell, Sarit charmed her CEO and CBO (Chief Business Officer) in her company and impressed them with her potential. It took her a year to convince them that she was ready to shift into a Business Development (BD) role, rather than a scientific leadership role. After a year of apprenticing, learning, tagging along and contributing in BD meetings, the CEO and CBO said, "You're ready." They gave her the opportunity to play the key go-to role putting a business deal together. The objective was to in-license a discovery that was co-owned by a private government-backed investor group, an academic institution and an inventor/entrepreneur with a mercurial temperament and a larger-than-life persona. None of them trusted each other. The science looked promising. And Sarit's company was in a great position to develop and commercialize their asset. But the delicate politics, egos, fears and competing business interests of the three owners of the Intellectual Property made it a complex deal to put together.

Sarit's crisis started on a Friday afternoon, when she was preparing her ad-hoc BD team for a key meeting with the IP owners. Suddenly, the CEO threw open the door and stomped into the conference room. "Are you the one running this deal?" the CEO asked Sarit with a glare and a sarcastic and sneering chuckle. Everyone looked down, like a planeload of passengers avoiding eye contact with a terrorist. Sarit stared at the CEO, stunned into speechlessness. Her face grew hot and, if she were light-skinned, her cheeks would have turned beet red. The CEO pressed on, annoyed that she didn't get a quicker and snappier answer. "My question wasn't rhetorical," she said. "Don't look at me with goat eyes. Tell me. Who is actually running this deal?"

This wasn't the first time the CEO had barged into a room, put someone on the spot, stunned them into speechlessness and then got annoyed and impatient when they didn't respond to her accusatory query with brilliance. She was clearly leading somewhere, and neither Sarit nor anyone on her ad-hoc BD team knew what the big boss actually wanted. The tension in the room grew more palpable with every second of silence, as the CEO stood at the front of the conference room waiting for an answer. "I guess I'm supposed to be running this deal," Sarit finally answered, sheepishly.

"That's exactly right," the CEO answered, taking Sarit's answer as an invitation to vent her fury at Sarit and the entire BD team. "If you're running this deal, what should happen if someone speaks up and gives you ideas that could put the deal in jeopardy?" This time, the question was rhetorical. The CEO didn't give Sarit a chance to respond, before she launched into a lecture. "If you're running the deal, that's different from 'just following orders.' If you're running the deal, you're supposed to vet ideas, even if they come from the CEO or from a member of our board. You're supposed to treat your superiors as a resource, seek our input and listen to what we have to say. But I shouldn't hear from a consultant or from a board member that you think my style of negotiating is going to create a mess and let this asset get away from us. Especially if you see things I have overlooked and if you have better ideas that can get us where we want to go. Putting this deal together will take brilliance, not 'doing what the boss says and hoping it gets us where we need to go.'"

Sarit blinked back tears. This was her first big BD assignment – and was a pivot point opportunity that could make or break her career advancement. She desperately wanted it to be a "wow" success. She wanted everyone to be happy with her work. Now, it seemed, she was damned no matter what she did. How do you Power Up your Brilliance and keep a micro-managing, hands-on, reluctant-to-delegate CEO happy when the directions she gives you are clearly wrong, when she doesn't see what she doesn't see and insists that you do things her way? Reject her ideas and there's hell to pay. Accept her ideas and you're a scapegoat when things turn sour and the very risks you predicted come home to roost.

Catch-22s, double binds and schizophrenogenic parenting

In families, as in enterprises, negativity, gotchas and hyper-critical micro-managing erode courage and paralyze those who receive repeated belittling. Catch-22s and double binds stifle initiative. Epidemiological studies trace the origins of addiction, of debilitating anxieties, of paranoid delusions and other debilitating mental illnesses. In most cases, some powerful "higher-ups" in a family system behave like Sarit's CEO. Others, like Sarit's CBO, stand by passively, make excuses and enable the abuse. Non-nurturing parents, aunts, uncles, older siblings or cousins may not be crazy themselves. Nor are the bystanders. But epidemiological studies label them "schizophrenogenic," because their rants, demands and lack of nurturing make others around them crazy. They often are oblivious to the fear they create, like the pilot of a speedboat who doesn't look back and doesn't see how his/her wake destabilizes everything in its energy path.

Recent research on the epidemiology of mental illness has taken a different path. These studies ask about resilience, rather than pathology (Neenan, 2009; Seligman, 2012). How do many people manage to stay happy and flourish, despite being exposed to the same negativity, rants, taunts and toxic family dynamics that are crazy-making for others? And, for those who regain their courage, what is it that therapy equips them to do?

We raised this question with my cousin, Leah, who is the most courageous and resilient person we've ever met. Leah is an 90-year-old Holocaust survivor, living alone in a modest garden apartment near the old city square in Netanya, Israel. Two weeks before we first met Leah, we visited the Hungarian History Museum in Budapest, where a curious docent overheard our family conversation and provided a few missing clues about the location of our grandfather's village, which had changed names when the borders were redrawn before and after World War II. When we logged onto the Yad Yashem website, entered the Klein family name and the Czech name for my grandfather's village, we got a hit. That hit connected us to our cousin, Leah.

"How did you survive" we asked her, "and how did you make your way to Israel?" Leah laughed and her eyes gleamed as she answered. "Guts," she said, in Hebrew. She explained how she refused to be a victim. How she stayed alert for opportunities. How she kept her sister and a childhood friend close and looked out for them. How the sisters created their own luck. How they warmed the hearts of others and touched their altruistic and nurturing instincts – so, knowing it was illegal, sympathetic villagers kept them alive, supplied them with morsels of food, a place to sleep, a kind word and lied to the police, lest they find the burned-out house they were using as a hiding place. Leah focused her defiance on flourishing, not merely surviving. And on Powering Up her Brilliance.

Before we drove to Netanya to visit Leah, friends warned us not to expect too much. For most families, reunions like ours are not pleasant. They're more like the painful, guilt-ridden, joyless "where-were-you-when-I-needed-you-and-what-will-you-do-for-me-now" encounters depicted in the movie, *Avalon* (2001), rather than a happily-every-after relationship. We were blessed with Leah. From the first moment we entered her living room, we were greeted with kisses and smiles, tears of joy, with positive recollection of how much my face looks like my grandfather's, whom she remembered vividly from his visit to the old family village, along with my grandmother, in the years before the Nazi occupation. Years later, our visits with Leah continue to be a source of joy and celebration – something, she tells us, is her last act of defiance and of courage. She enriches our lives deeply.

So – what is Leah's secret? And, when Sarit shuts down and complains about "feeling like a duck in an arcade," because of the constant barrage of criticism she receives, what can she learn from Leah — and that bolster her courage?

Look inside yourself to flip the switch on the 5 Activators

Courage is a paradox. We admire it in resilient team leaders like Sarit and heroes like our Cousin Leah. But none of us would want to walk in their shoes and endure the adversities that tested their mettle. We hope we have that extra power boost in reserve, like an insurance policy that we buy and hope we never need to use.

Yet, activation — to Power Up Brilliance and ignite the sgAAC in our brains, is a skill, not a trait, that we can practice when we feel the pinch of pressure, stress, adversity. It's a choice that takes practice before it becomes a conditioned near-automatic reflex. It may take a reminder, an icon, a formula that signals us to look East, West, North, South and Deep — and find our Activators — rather than waiting until a boss, customer, board or external forces intervenes and creates conditions that are ideal.

Tap energy from the East. Muster the Will to step up and take charge. Choose whatever mantra works. Maybe it's remembering John Wayne's classic quote, "Yep, you're afraid. Saddle up anyway, partner."

Merom Klein & Louise Yochee Klein

Maybe it's hearing the song, *High Hopes,* about the ant that moved a rubber tree plant. Maybe it's the pep-talk you got from a parent, Army officer or coach, before a big audition or a big play. Maybe it's Leah's defiance or the audacity of hope that emboldens you when you face old prejudices about "what women or people of color can and cannot achieve." Or a breathing, meditation and mental-alertness training, that can bring down your blood pressure so you don't tear up, turn red or get flustered when the boss stomps in and gives you a piece of her mind. Choose whatever gets you to be a fearful *non*-retreater, with a can-do attitude, confidence and joy about lifting your head above the parapets. Like Sarit, you may see your career with the company flash in front of your eyes and may feel your heart beating in your throat. But that doesn't have to shut you down, if you choose to sharpen your awareness, energize yourself and lift your game. Or, as positive psychology guru Martin Seligman calls says, "if you choose to flourish."

Align your compass North. Stay focused on Purpose. Keep the noise in the background, so it doesn't make you forget what you're there to do — and what you're actually accountable to achieve. Job One, for Sarit, was getting the deal done. If the CEO gets worried and wonders whether Sarit is pushing as hard and thinking as innovatively as she can, Sarit again has a choice. She can get insulted and indignant (which will do nothing to allay her CEO's concerns and quell the noise). Or, she can reassure a panicked CEO that she "gets" what's important for enterprise-success, and that their interests and priorities are aligned. So can you, when you have to say, "No," or "Not now" to a sponsor who tells you what to do, but doesn't have an orchestrator's

Use the 5 Courage Activators as Your Roadmap

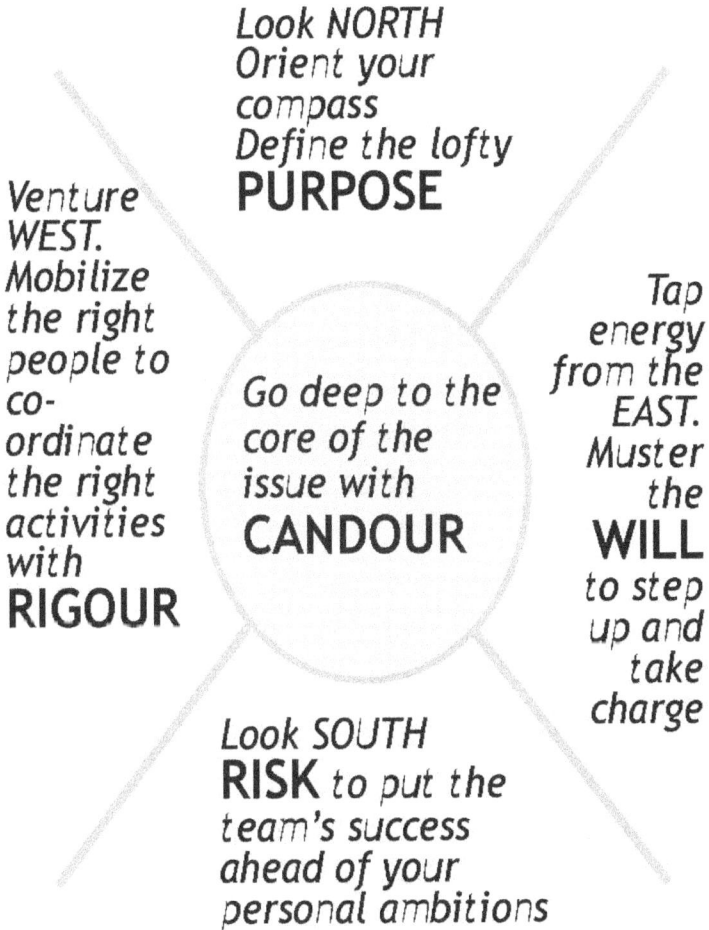

Look NORTH
Orient your
compass
Define the lofty
PURPOSE

Venture
WEST.
Mobilize
the right
people to
co-
ordinate
the right
activities
with
RIGOUR

Go deep to the
core of the
issue with
CANDOUR

Tap
energy
from the
EAST.
Muster
the
WILL
to step
up and
take
charge

Look SOUTH
RISK to put the
team's success
ahead of your
personal ambitions

peripheral vision. And who herself is getting fearful and anxious and losing sight of what really has to get done.

Go deep to the center. Open Candor. Our friend Dr Andrea Zintz (2011) suggests a technique that she and her research collaborators call "adaptive inquiry" — to engage emotions like worry, panic, frustration, hurt or anger, rather than trying to silence or neutralize an antagonist's opposition. Suppose Sarit had done that, when the CEO barged into the conference room. "You must be really worried to ask a question like that, and tell us all that it isn't rhetorical," Sarit might have said, in a calming voice. "What's your concern?" With open questions, adaptive inquiry sparks a generative, solution-seeking, creative dialogue to ignite brilliance. It's a simple formula. Customer service reps are trained to use it all the time, to get out of the parent-to-child/child-to-parent power hierarchy with angry customers who've lost luggage, had claims denied, or inadvertently mangled their hard-drives – and manage the interaction, so it becomes adult-to-adult problem-solving instead. With some practice and coaching, so could Sarit. And you. You might be able to infuse it with some humour as well, to infuse the situation with a more positive energy and Will.

Look South. Risk to put team ahead of self. Teams accomplished more if orchestrators like Sarit aren't concerned who gets credit for the big idea or who gets promoted or bonused for the team's success. Having the right reward system helps. But a trusting rather than risk-averse mental perspective helps even more. As problems arise, Sarit could show a desire to help, not blame. She could get out in front of the egos, anxieties, entitlements and interests that could be put at risk to build trust and ask directly for the support and benefit of the doubt she needs. She could show her willingness to defer personal ambitions and to go the extra kilometre to take care of sensitive team members. And, if they balk or ask for too much, she could backtrack — to Will, Purpose and Candor — and negotiate for the support she needs.

Venture West. And wrestle down the right issues with Rigor. This is where Sarit was when the CEO barged into the room. She'd brought together the right luminaries — synchronously (in their live huddle in the conference room) and asynchronously (by soliciting ideas and generating adaptive dialogue via emails and web-exchanges, with tools like GroupMind Express and Basecamp). She knew who had what expertise to offer and what they could contribute to the best BD strategy and its smooth execution, with stepping stones, interdependencies, costs and accountabilities defined. She had a plan. But the plan would take Risk to embrace, Candor to refine, Purpose to depoliticize "who does what" and "who decides what," and Will to look past fear — when there are bumps, barriers and setbacks. Collectively, these Power Up Brilliance to innovate and improvise. In partnership with the CEO.

A systemwide perspective to transcend hierarchy traps

Barry Oshry (2007) designed a leadership training simulation that he calls the PowerLab. It dramatizes the Catch 22s and double binds that test the courage of middle-level Orchestrators like Sarit, as they influence up, manage down and mobilize peers at their same level.

In Oshry's PowerLab simulation, players are divided into three levels — Tops, Middles and Bottoms. The Tops are told what the investors and regulators expect. Bottoms are given the tools and the playing field. The Middles are the Orchestrators. In most groups, it takes only 20 minutes for most the Middles to feel as paralyzed and as under attack as Sarit — and for brilliance to be squelched.

The key, Oshry observed, is the way that Tops deal with performance pressure — and the way that Middles respond when Tops get worried, frightened, threatened, and telegraph their lack of confidence to the Middles who work under their supervision.

The Middle is not an easy place to be. Tops are often demanding, critical and withholding. Bottoms often go rogue, or wait passively for "take-us-by-the-hand" direction, rather than taking initiative and using their own good judgment. And the politics can be fierce, as other Middles jockey for position, for special favor or for a huge allocation of resources. To anyone who's ever been in Sarit's position, the pressures that Middles face in the simulation are all too real.

In the simulation, as in life, Middles have a choice. They can get caught in what Oshry calls "the hierarchy trap" — and respond to the Tops' fear by cow-towing, freezing, rebelling or disengaging and by becoming a shadow of their leaders, managing down the same way they are managed. In the hierarchy trap, Middles become more fixated on following orders than taking initiative, more fixated on pleasing the boss rather than getting results, more fixated on making Bottoms feel secure rather than challenging them to do better, more fixated on acquiring power rather than mobilizing others in a way that is empowering.

With practice and perspective, Middles can acquire the courage to break free of hierarchy traps. It starts with the awareness that hierarchy traps are not imposed. They are a choice. The choice starts with the perspective you take, when the pressure increases, nerves get frayed and tempers get hot.

"Stuff happens," Oshry wrote, commenting on the dynamics that occur when Tops get worried and when Bottoms go rogue or acquiesce passively. "You can choose to take it personally or treat it systemically." Taking it personally leaves Orchestrators feeling like victims who blame others for "causing" the discomfort that they experience. They keep their heads below the parapets, safely out of the line of fire, relegated to a place on the sidelines rather than putting themselves into the Center of the action. In the PowerLab — and in real life, when you are supposed to be "running a deal" — viewing power dynamics from a victim's perspective is the worst thing that an Orchestrator like Sarit can do.

What's their worst fear? We don't often think of Tops living in fear — any more than, as children, we think of parents having their own struggles and vulnerabilities or needing our encouragement. When Sarit recognized that her CEO was afraid rather than oppressive or dysfunctional, she saw more ways to take control of her storming-in, deflect her barbs, and reassure her that things are on-track. And to push back and challenge, when the CEO tried to help by saying, "Here's what to do," but was actually costing rather than scoring points.

Ask any clinician and they'll tell you that fear, pain and defensiveness are the biggest challenges in patient management. You have to anesthetize the nerves before you can do a root canal or distract needle-phobic patients before giving an injection. And equip the family to cope, when they see a loved one in pain. Skilled Orchestrators also need a good bedside manner, when the operation they are running will take some team members out of their comfort or security zones.

Greasing more than the squeaky wheel. A Chief Medical Officer had a sign prominently displayed in his office that announced, "Our discussion will go better if you bring two good system-wide solutions rather than one parochial problem." Rather than micro-managing, like Sarit's CEO, he expected Orchestrators to take initiative, listen to Advisors, see what Executors needed and bring forward their very best, not necessarily the easiest or most obvious solutions.

Those closest to the job may, as the axiom says, have the best insight about what's needed to do the job. They may have interesting solutions. But they may not know what other jobs are being done in parallel, or what's happening upstream or downstream from where they sit. Orchestrators like Sarit need to listen to outspoken, perhaps high-maintenance, stakeholders like the inventor of the technology — and then use good judgment to figure out what's best to run the deal, not just appease those who push hard and champion their interests.

When people are rational and objective, this is hard enough. But when Executors and Advisors are afraid that their jobs could be redefined, or even gone, in tomorrow's portfolio review or re-organization — or when they're not given a clear line of sight into the reasoning behind those decisions — it's hard for Orchestrators to convince them to go "above and beyond" what's required to co-ordinate their efforts. They may leave emails unanswered, ignore instructions or compromise on specifications that won't matter until the project moves a few more steps downstream. They may go out for lunch or home for the long holiday weekend, unconcerned about the reverberations of a delay through the enterprise. Or may reply to "what if…?" questions by telling you what they know, rather than what they imagine, invent, deduce or concoct, to create an inflection point that will take the enterprise further than "the way we've always done things."

It's lonely in the middle

Sarit felt torn. As the person in the middle, it felt like she had to choose between pleasing her CEO and pleasing her team, between pleasing her company or caving in to pressure from a demanding inventor. The last time Sarit could remember feeling this way was when she was going back and forth between her estranged parents. Each had their own set of needs, priorities, idiosyncrasies. Saying "Yes" to one meant that Sarit would have to say, "No" or "Not now" to the other. The more irreconcilable the demands were, the more Sarit felt forced to take sides, when each parent demanded to know where her loyalties truly were. She felt that same lump in her throat in the BD orchestration role — when each side expected her to be "their" advocate and protector.

The more you care, the more contentious the issue is and the more you can see everyone's positions — as well as the system wide implications — the more torn you feel when you mediate among competing factions, interests, perspectives when you do shuttle diplomacy. Beg, borrow, allocate and re-allocate resources – like some corporate Robin Hood, who finds bandwidth and capital in one part of the system and commandeers it for another initiative, project team or customer to do their job. When you are a chameleon, changing colors and perspectives so often that no one can ever tell where "the real you" stands. When you're torn, you're expected to stay level-headed and emotionally giving, even when none of the factions or interests you're orchestrating rise above their narrow perspectives and self-interests. It means you're the adult. And that you'll have to answer tough, sometimes accusatory or belittling, questions, when saying "Yes" to one group of interests means that you'll have to say "No" or "Not now" to someone else — or wait to get back to them altogether.

Ask anyone who's a child of estranged parents. They'll tell you about low-courage Power-Down Brilliance options to escape from feeling torn. They can take one person's side and demonize the other. They can compromise rather than optimize. They can withdraw. Or privately agree with each party who lobbies them for support, without ever taking a stand or committing to a decision. The larger and more complex the enterprise is, the more places there are to hide in the matrix, delegate upward, and keep the issue "in play," while keeping your head below the parapets. The more people there are to consult, the more you can do wave after wave of blue-sky, feel-good, possibility-thinking brainstorming, without ever flipping the switch on critical thinking, weighing alternatives, pressure-testing opposing ideas and committing to a decision.

Stepping up and "running the deal," without allowing yourself to be emotionally blackmailed or browbeaten, requires courage. Not only from Sarit, but also from the Sponsors who see what is unfolding, and who see the emotional toll that tearing takes. A benign grandparent, aunt or uncle, older sibling or cousin or family friend might try to spare a child from the tearing she experiences when she's trying to mediate between estranged parents at the Christmas or Passover dinner table. With the same care, a benign boss or mentor might want to shield Orchestrators like Sarit from Catch-22s and double binds, insulate them from conflicts, or absolve them of their fiduciary responsibilities. That's a lot more comfortable (and comforting) than straight talk that equips Sarit to "run the deal" in an adult-adult way, to step up and take charge of contentious issues. But protection doesn't advance Sarit's career — or give her the practice she needs to stand in the middle, where it admittedly can be lonely.

Six levels of brilliance: Assessing readiness

Parent-to-child vs adult-to-adult perspectives are not black-or-white alternatives. Anyone who's a careful observer of brilliance — as a dealmaker, a leader, a mentor or as business psychologists, like we are — knows that there are shades of grey. And that the courage to step up and stand in the middle, can rise and fall, until Orchestrators like Sarit master their personal triggers and make it sustainable.

"Start where the other person is, not where you want them to be." In 1975, Herb Shepard first espoused that rule of thumb for change agents and orchestrators. It's just as true today. Starting where they are doesn't mean that you'll leave them where they are. But it does mean that you've got to understand their reality, their fears, their sensitivities and hardships or risk polarizing your audience and turning a good number of them against you, like Dr C did when he said unsympathetically, "March or die."

Here's a chart that lists 6 levels of brilliance from low to high. Fortunately, these don't work like the Kubler-Ross stages of grief. There's no lock-step formula that says you have to go through all of these steps — or that you can't go back, if something triggers you in a way that evokes new fears or that gives you a new and different challenge. But knowing where you are — at any time — can tell you which of the Activators you need to pull you out of a victim-perspective, like Sarit's, when her CEO demanded to know "who's running the deal." And help you step up and take charge.

Denial. Business psychiatrist Judith Bardwick (2007) warned that people who start from a position of comfort and entitlement often do not react positively when they are shaken out of their slumber and asked to awaken to new realities. At best, they may be skeptical — and may hit the button and seek another few minutes, hours or years of slumber. They may ask you to justify your demands and debate your business case. Or may come out on the attack, like some disgruntled employees did when Dr C explained new business realities and said, "March or die."

Singer-songwriter John Gorka calls it "being born into ignorance and

Six Brilliance Levels

When You Encounter Setbacks or Obstacles

Levels of brilliance you might see when you ask others to stretch

When luminaries ask others to stretch beyond tried-and-true, business-as-usual solutions, they hope others will appreciate their brilliance and follow their lead. What if some followers are below the fear line, stuck in denial, blame or procrastination? To power up brilliance, luminaries have to diagnose their follower's level of support — without taking rejection, ridicule or sceptism personally — to uplift, ennoble and power up the brilliance they need.

TAKE-CHARGE, ENGAGE TRANSCEND FEAR

Level 5. CHAMPION: Teach it, advocate it, sell it
Who else should adopt it? • How do we scale up? • Where else could it add value?

Level 4. MASTERY: Learn it, do it, innovate, improve, get on with it!
What best practices? • What if we… • Let's take action". Let's get it done

Level 3. PLAN/MOBILIZE: Own it, step in, initiate, embrace it, act
Here's the plan • What could help? • Let's reach out to… • How do we start?

VICTIM, FIGHT-FLIGHT INDULGE FEAR

Level 2. WAIT/PROCRASTINATE: Talk it, delay, wait, comply
Let's wait until… • Time will take care of it • As you wish • I am almost ready

Level 1. BLAME: Fight it, argue, debate, ridicule
It's their fault • You don't appreciate • It's impossible to… • This is why

Level 0. DENIAL: Avoid it, ignore, rationalise, trivialise
This will pass • We're OK already • Not our job • No one else complained

privilege." Putting your head in the sand. Believing that effort, just following orders, keeping yourself Teflon-covered and conflict-free will be enough to advance your career and sustain your success. Pretending not to know what you don't want to know. Operating with a lack of Purpose, Will, Rigor, Risk and Candor Being at the top of the Maslow hierarchy, where your material, safety, security and status needs are fulfilled — and there is no sense of adversity, of stretch or challenge.

High-energy and a strong work ethic don't mean that team members have the courage to lift themselves out of denial, according to Bardwick (1995). Take Sarit's BD team, as an example. They were creative, engaged, turned on and firing on all cylinders, working hard to get the deal done. But the CEO saw them careening into a train wreck, by appeasing, giving away the store and responding congenially to terms that a responsible board would never approve. Might the CEO have delivered her warning in a more artful, ennobling way? Of course. But imagine how the trajectory might have changed if Sarit had gotten over the sting and said something like this to her team — and to herself to Power Up Brilliance:

> "I know we're working hard and doing our best and it doesn't feel good to be told, 'This isn't good enough — yet.' But our CEO is telling us that we've got to lift our game because this deal won't fly, in the way that it's coming together. Let's suppose she's right. What new benchmarks could we establish for ourselves?"

Blame. At the second courage level, your antagonist gets the Purpose and may even have the Candor to acknowledge there's room for improvement.

But that doesn't mean that s/he sees what can be done differently when you ask, "How could we achieve the new benchmarks?" Or believes that she should be the one to change course, or make an extra effort.

At this low level of brilliance, the parties are locked into a cycle of accusation and counter-accusation, fault-finding, we-versus-them defensiveness. Each faction can tell you why "it's not my fault" and can show you "why we're already doing the best that we can." The lines are drawn. And quite often, as we saw between Sarit and her CEO, the attacks get personal. As long as the dialogue gets stuck at this level, the best you can hope for is compromise. "What's the minimum that the other faction will accept?" becomes the guiding question when the team is stuck in Blame, not "What's the best way to get this deal done?"

Lifting the team out of this we-versus-them, win/lose, attack/counter-attack, stalemate requires an infusion of Risk especially at the very time that benefit of the doubt, mutuality, entrusting your success to someone else seems like too much for a reasonable person to ask. It isn't easy to fend off the temptation to fight back, go on the defensive and lift the parties above the politics, when you're the one feeling insulted or attacked. Or to refuse to take sides and bring antagonists together, rather than having them face off against each other.

How could Sarit have intervened, rather than keeping her head down, seething silently and wishing the conflict away? Imagine how the trajectory might have changed if she had said, "Let's take this off-line," when the CEO barged into the conference room and launched her attacks. And if, in private, she had said to her CEO:

"Listen, I know you're frustrated and worried. Me too. My career is on the line with this deal. I get it. I'm happy to step up, take charge and run the deal, and take your criticism and suggestions on-board. Help us do our job and bring the team together."

Procrastination. Catharsis. Insight. Great ideas. Deep conversation. Clever breakthrough plans. These are the consultation hours that are especially gratifying for psychologist, coach, facilitator or project manager. Especially when they're spiced up with laughter. Until the next consultation, when you have the same conversation again — and find that nothing has really been done to act on the advice that was taken to heart. Purpose? You bet. Candor? Yes. Risk? We say we're all on the same team. But there's no Will to put the pedal to the metal, give it some juice and shift from neutral into gear to get traction.

Of course, there are always valid reasons for your antagonist to procrastinate. Competing priorities. Adversities. Political vulnerabilities. Support that failed to materialize. Other people who didn't do what they promised to do, when they promised to do it, and who say, simply, "I forgot." There are Second thoughts. Temptations. Distractions.

What could Sarit do to activate a reluctant or fearful antagonist's Will? It starts with recognizing Procrastination for what it is rather than giving in and accepting the excuses. With a pep-talk and an expression of "you-can-do-it" confidence. An affirmation of values. A statement of solidarity that says, "We're in this together." And a provocative question like:

"I'm curious. Help me understand. You say you're with the program and want to help us make this happen. But every time we're about to pull the trigger, something else comes up to get in the way. What can we do to lift your urgency? How can we shift the momentum and make it less difficult? And, if not now, when?"

Engagement. Now the magic starts to happen, because the partner you are mobilizing "gets it" and is ready to "get on with it." With Candor added to the mix of the 5 Activators, the ideas flow. There's a sense of camaraderie, of being in it together — whether you're all under one roof in the same sales team, laboratory or factory, or whether you're a virtual team for the next 15-20 minutes on a conference call or blog exchange. You're accountable to one another and don't want to let the team down by breaking your commitments. You're playing off of each others' energy, piggy-backing on one another's ideas, more concerned with what gets done rather than who gets the credit. Criticism? Your state of mind says, "Bring it on. Sharpen me up. Let's pressure-test our ideas before we run into problems that we might have foreseen and prevented."

Research on creativity shows that there's a world of difference between idea-generation and culling through to choose what's the best fit and honing ideas to convert them into practical and workable innovations. According to creativity guru Ed DeBono, they put on different thinking hats. According to research by John Lehrer on creativity, these different "hats" or problem-solving practices activate different chemical processes in the brain. Idea generation, which wears Ed DeBono's (1999) green and yellow thinking hats, is fun, upbeat, pleasurable. It releases endorphins. And lifts Will.

But risk identification, critical thinking and risk mitigation, which wear Ed DeBono's black and white hats, are the places where Will is put to the test. They require a different kind of concentration. Evoke different feelings. Critical thinking brings down your mood, even with the healthiest of team dynamics and the most motivated thought-leaders. It's why so many books are unfinished, so many symphonies unarranged, so many scripts are unedited and unrefined.

So, Sarit, if you're going to get people engaged in the uphill climb and heavy lifting of innovation and creativity, as well as the turn-on and fun part, you've got to give your team a running start. Let them know what lies ahead, and that it's a normal part of the creative process, rather than something dysfunctional. Take fear, humiliation, embarrassment, threats out of the equation so good judgment doesn't become judgmental, as our friend and colleague Andrea Zintz says. And use the metaphor of switching in and out of different hats, so it's clear that we won't be stuck in the world of black and white forever.

Mastery. Finally, at this level, you've arrived. You've brought the right parties together. Imbued them with Purpose, Risk, Will and Candor— or have been fortunate enough to inherit a collection of individuals who came forward with their own inner strengths and inner voices, activating courage for themselves. The ground is plowed, fertilized and ready for Rigor — the sweet spot for innovation, improvisation, creativity, problem-solving, and for refining, fine-tuning, honing, upgrading the ideas you generated and the plans that looked good when they first were posted on your blog or sketched out on the back of a napkin.

Our colleague Rod Napier has built a career on designing group structures that give teams the Rigor to move from the feel-good world of brainstorming and appreciative inquiry into tough rigorous world of pressure-testing ideas, weighing alternatives, challenging assumptions, giving and getting feedback. To sharpen up each other's thinking in a way that builds, rather than erodes, the foundations of shared Purpose, open Candor, resilient Will, and trusting Risk — without a Steve Jobs or Dov Frohman to play the role of critical parent. So orchestrators, regardless of level or professional background, pull a standing team or ad-hoc task force together and ennoble them to solve today's vexing problems and seize or create tomorrow's opportunities.

Rod's classic books, *Group: Theory and Experience* (2004), *Measuring What Matters* (2006), *Advanced Games for Trainers* (1999), *Intentional Design and the Process of Change* (2002), *High Impact Tools and Activities for Strategic Planning* (1997), offer "how-to-do-it" guides that can be adapted for large and small groups meeting face-to-face, or for any number of stakeholders invited to an online asynchronous debate. Tools like GroupMind Express provide not only a place for brainstorming and idea generation, but a platform for the heavy lifting, grinding and hot messy work that's involved to move from a bountiful harvest to a nutritious sustainable diet.

What one word does Rod use over and over again, like a mantra, with experienced Orchestrators who've run into new challenges and with newbies like Sarit? Design. Put people together in the right configurations, ask them the right questions in the right order, use time compression and time limits, drive toward data-driven, outcome-based rather than "who's-got-power-dictates" decision-making and you've got a recipe for robust, even heated, debate where the issues are taken seriously and the ideas are pressure-tested mercilessly, but egos and personalities are unharmed.

There's no shortage of innovation-fostering techniques: Storyboarding, fish-bone analysis, DeBono's six hats (2008), force-field analysis, The FIRE method (Mckinney, 2012), 15% solutions, positive deviance (Pascale, Sternin and Sternin, 2010), adaptive inquiry (Zintz and Jones, 2012), scenario building, crowdsourcing, story-boarding, think inside-the-box creativity, Stage-Gate innovation. Just as there's no shortage of tools on the shelf if you walk into a home center store. No matter which tools you pull off the shelf and use, in Sarit's role as an Orchestrator or as an Advisor who's party to the deliberations, you'll face the same test of courage head-on. You'll need Rigor to stay with the process and to see it through until the pragmatics are wrestled down and converted into action plans, GANTT charts, timelines and assigned accountabilities.

Champion. The last rung on the ladder is more than being an artisan yourself, a master craftsperson who can mobilize and orchestrate and Power Up Brilliance. It's spreading what you know how to do. Getting others onboard. Showing them how to put it all together to make it work and pull it off. To woo and wow the audiences, end-users, beneficiaries whose lives you want to enrich to make a difference and monetize the discoveries, good ideas and inventions you've produced. It's where all 5 Activators come together — like the smooth firing of a 5-cylinder turbo-charged engine — to power you up the hill, around the curve, across the desert or through the snow.

Once more – the courage to Power Up is a paradox

When you're at mastery — or, above it, as a champion — you may break a sweat when the going gets tough. It may take a super effort. But the challenges and adversities that looked daunting or overwhelming at Blame, Procrastination, Engagement and Improvisation no longer evoke fear. The ground below seems solid. Sure, there's turbulence, but like the rocking of you feel on a familiar railroad, you know how to flex your knees, roll with the bumps and stay on your feet. And Power Up Brilliance.

If you are Sarit's CEO, you've seen a dozen deals like this before — and you have a sixth sense, to know when your BD team is on-track or off-the-rails, like a skilled pilot who knows in an instant, what has to be done to lift out of a stall or fly through a storm. You can read the cues, making the trajectory of the trendline predictable, not random. You know what levers you can pull and what contingencies and back-ups you need to have ready just-in-case. No wonder it's called your comfort zone, strike zone, sweet spot. Even when it's hard work.

Enjoy the feeling of mastery. But don't allow yourself to get complacent. Because one thing is sure. Sooner or later, today's Mastery will become tomorrow's Denial. The negotiating tactics that worked a year ago may not be effective with a new generation of partners, any more than the flying that kept a Piper Cub in the air will work with a 787. Today's Mastery got you here. It begins the cycle that tests your courage all over again, at new inflection points. For most of us, that will be much sooner than we'd like, and we'll be tempted to Blame or shoot the messenger, just as Sarit's CEO was tempted to do when Sarit said, "We know that worked for you before. But this situation calls for something different. What worked before won't be innovative or brilliant enough to get this new deal done."

Chapter 7
Ennobling Dialogues to Power Up Brilliance

It's no secret that human conversation has uplifting and healing powers. Why else would the all-powerful Pharaoh, in the very cradle of civilization, allow an itinerant Hebrew like Joseph to hang around, interpret his dreams and offer counsel? Why else would talk-therapy be effective treating anxieties and depression, and would sports psychologists help athletes run faster, push harder and throw more accurately? It's no different for us than it was for the ancient Egyptian Pharaoh or a superstar football player. How we interpret our adversities determines, in large measure, whether we'll perish or Power Up Brilliance to flourish.

In a series of studies in the 1960s, elementary school teachers were told that a select group of first grader students, chosen at random, had unusually high potential. The teachers were unaware of any differences in the way they related to the so-called high-potentials vs average or low-potential students in their classes. But researchers Robert Rosenthal and Lenore Jacobson tracked the teachers' words, gestures, voice tone and bandwidth. Capturing interactions on videotape and in live classroom observations, Rosenthal and Jacobson discovered subtle, but powerful, differences in the way teachers related to students who supposedly had potential — and saw how those differences lifted or suppressed the students' performance. The studies, reported by Professor Robert Rosenthal and Lenore Jacobson (1968, 2003), have been replicated with adults and children of other ages, with soldiers and civilians, across cultures, even with laboratory mice being trained by experimenters to run mazes.

In another classic series of studies, conducted at the Hawthorne Works in the 1920s, experimenters wanted to see what conditions would have the most positive impact on performance. They turned the lights up and performance increased. Then, they turned the lights down and performance increased a bit more. They turned the heat up and down and each time a change was introduced, performance increased. Social psychologist John French looked at the conflicting results and got an "Aha!" It wasn't conditions per se, it was the attention that the workers received that made the difference. When someone noticed the workers and was interested in how conditions would affect them, their performance improved. French (1953) termed it "the Hawthorne effect." Even unwittingly, the experimenters Powered Up Brilliance with factory workers in the 1920s — transmitting the belief that they had "the right stuff" to grab hold of a change in working conditions and lift their performance.

Of course, truly brilliant performance isn't created by some passive transfusion from a dispassionate observer or true believer to someone who's receiving their beneficence. Recent research data on top performers, or outliers, assembled and reported by Malcolm Gladwell (2008), shows that truly brilliant performers work hard to take advantage of the attention, opportunity, feedback they're given. Gladwell talks about the ice-time that physically more advanced hockey players get, Bill Gates' access to the computer lab at Harvard, the Beatles' stage-time as the house band in Hamburg Germany. He talks about the encouragement, tough love, reinforcement and stimulation that bolstered their courage and gave them the grit to go the distance and do "whatever it took" to succeed. He also talks about the 10,000+ hours of grit, determination, hard work, trial-and-error practice that it took for any of these outliers to hone their skills, get their chops up and develop themselves from high-potentials into high-achievers. And about the jeers, criticism, temptation they had to endure, long before there was any glitz or glamour.

Soon after her song, *From a Distance,* won a Grammy for Best Song of the Year, singer-songwriter Julie Gold spoke to a hometown audience in Philadelphia about her meteoric rise to success. She talked about the ten years of perseverance that it took to stay in the game, to keep networking and getting to the right people, before success "just happened." Her lesson, which she offered to the audience? Keep at it. Renew your enthusiasm. Stay resilient. Manage your courage. Similarly, listen to successful entrepreneurs like Andrew Pearlman, founder and CEO of Medgenics, who persevered for 10 years of heavy lifting before seeing his enterprise take off; Chiang Li, founder and CEO of Boston Biomedical, which he funded from his own life savings after failing to raise venture capital; Yossi Vardi, founder of no less than a dozen Israeli high-tech ventures, each of which required endurance to overcome the head wind blowing against success; or read the amalgamation of studies about "the entrepreneurial mindset" assembled by Rita McGrath (2000). They'll tell you that the key to success is to keep yourself in the game, with the flexibility to keep learning and adjusting your game plan when Plan A and Plan B and Plan C aren't taking you where you want to go. And to listen to those who will help you sharpen up and lift your game, and ignore those who tell you to throw in the towel and give it up altogether.

So, with centuries of anecdotal evidence and decades of experimental data all showing how important encouragement is to success, among schoolchildren and adults, entrepreneurs and good soldiers, even among laboratory mice running mazes for pellets of food, we find it strange when someone asks, "Can courage really be learned?" The answer is obvious. Of course it can. It takes is a coach, mentor, boss, project leader or partner to believe in you (or pretend to believe in you), and take the Risk to invest in your success. It takes them giving you the ice-time and opportunity. And, of course, it takes you to do your part and do them proud in the way that you seize the opportunity they give you.

Meet Amal — lots of talent, hard work, but a lack of courage

Amal is a gifted medicinal chemist. Before he joined the company as Head of Chemistry, he had a long list of patents to his credit. One of the drugs he discovered was on the market, albeit in a different formulation from the one he originally devised. The company was thrilled to attract someone with Amal's credentials, track record and brilliance. And, when Amal was asked why he joined such a small company, he replied that it was a thrill to be part of a group that was doing cutting-edge work, redefining drug discovery and that had so many promising compounds in its development pipeline.

As long as cross-functional teams gave Amal easy access to support functions and made his life easier, he was enthusiastic about the company's cross-functional matrix structure. But a crisis erupted when some of those same support functions stepped up, acted like advisors and pressed Amal and his medicinal chemists to rethink the chemical structure of the lead compound they were synthesizing. Amal was insulted. And was on a rampage to protect his honor — and the honor of his chemistry team.

"We are medicinal chemists, not short-order cooks!" he protested. "What cheek! Computational and analytic chemists have no idea what it takes to synthesize a novel molecule that binds to a receptor with a stable, therapeutically active, scalable formulation. If they ever try to critique us or give us a recipe again," Amal proclaimed, now shouting, "I will tell my entire chemistry team to walk out and stop working on any of their projects."

Amal repeated his impassioned appeal to anyone who would listen. When he finally had an audience with the CEO and Chief Technology Officer (CTO), he paused and waited for an apology, for affirmation of the medicinal chemists' pre-eminent hegemony, and for assurance that the CEO and CTO would not tolerate pressure and interference that could stifle his group's initiative and inventiveness. He was incredulous when they asked about the computational chemists' suggestions and extolled the virtues of dynamic tension among disciplines in a cross-functional team rather than automatically deferring to Amal and "his" medicinal chemists.

'This is so unfair," Amal said, trying to calm himself. "It is harassment, plan and simple. I cannot collude with this any more." With that said, Amal stormed out of the CEO's office and walked across the hall, insisting on an immediate audience with the Human Resources (HR) Director. He was ready to resign, right there and then, and was convinced that he had ample justification to sue the company for discrimination.

No one wanted to attack Amal or send him into a panic. Nor did they want his resignation. But the new drugs that his group was synthesizing were far more difficult than anything that the chemists had ever done before. Regulatory approval, reimbursement, safety and patent registration were also more difficult requiring disciplines to sharpen each other up, not leave each other alone. Amal thought he was doing the right thing by trying to protect himself and insulate his chemists against harsh and unfair criticism. He thought he was showing courage and brilliance, by taking charge and pushing others — distractors, detractors, critics — out of the way. But, in reality, he was "stuck" at Denial and Blame by refusing to let anyone give him feedback or lift his game higher. His righteous indignation and outrage was keeping the rest of his team stuck too.

Mindfulness: A moment of truth for any advisor

So, here you are, Amal's HR Director. It's a delicate situation. Amal is seated at your conference table, a scowl on his face, waiting to see how you'll accede to his demands. The last thing the enterprise needs is a Head of Chemistry on a work stoppage or a slow-down, threatening to sue. Or an open position that you've got to scramble to fill, while the clock is running on your timelines and you're burning through your R&D capital. Nor can you tolerate any Head of Function — especially one that's supposed to be at the very heart of innovation — eschewing cross-functional collaboration and saying, "my way or the highway." How do you cool the immediate crisis and assuage bruised egos, without turning the heat down on the scientific, technical and business debates that can accelerate progress and power real innovation?

It starts with your own inner dialogue. Do you see the dialogue with Amal as a distraction, an annoyance, a waste of your precious time and bandwidth? If so, it's a cinch that you'll telegraph your negative self-fulfilling prophecies even if you're convinced that you've disguised your true feelings. You'll be far more effective if you can flip your own inner switch, change your emotional channel and approach the dialogue with compassion, resolve, patience and with the understanding that lifting Amal out of his Denial and Blame isn't interfering with your job, because it *is* your job. Just like the schoolteachers did in Rosenthal's famous studies when they were convinced that their efforts would lift high-potential schoolchildren to new heights.

What if you can't get your heart and your head to that place that Boyatzis and McKee (2008) call mindfulness? What if you can't suspend judgment, stay in the "here-and-now," find compassion and connect with the best angels rather than the demons in an antagonist like Amal, at the times when he is beset with fear, reluctance, mistrust and other courage-inhibitors? What if you don't honestly believe he'll be able to lift his game? If you can't make the emotional investment to be "all-in" and mindful and to see your antagonist's potential, even when s/he is making you crazy, then you're better off making a referral — to a manager, mentor or external coach who can sustain this attention and intention, and pick up where you've given up.

From enabling to ennobling, sympathy to challenge

The 5 Power Up Activators give you a roadmap to uplift and engage a frightened, resistant or complacent antagonist like Amal, whether you are his HR Director, Project Manager, CEO or a key advisor with a seat on the Board of Directors. Open with sympathy, starting where your antagonist is rather than where you want him/her to be. Empathize. Acknowledge his/her fears and the adversities, real or imagined, imposed or self-created. Suspend judgment. Then get permission to challenge, lift, transcend, inspire and ignite brilliance to replace complacency and resignation. Find solutions. And drive toward execution, mobilizing the support that's needed to achieve breakthrough possibilities.

Here's what the dialogue sounded like, in real-time, when the HR Director ushered Amal into her office and closed the door, to talk about the crisis that had erupted. Even if you are not a HR professional, you too can follow the roadmap and, with a little practice, engage, uplift, ennoble and Power Up Brilliance:

Start North, with Purpose. It's tempting to start by commenting on Amal's outburst and reprimanding his unprofessional behavior. But the HR Director knew that throwing down the gauntlet, however justified, wouldn't put her and Amal on the same team, working toward a shared Purpose, but would polarize the dialogue and drive them into opposing camps. For that reason, she reigned in her incredulity and asked, "What were you hoping to accomplish with the ultimatum you gave our executive team?" In Amal's response, she hoped she'd hear something she could endorse, at least partially, so they could move forward on the same track.

Amal didn't let her down. He talked about the importance of doing top-flight scientific work and discovering best-in-class, first-in-class medicines. He talked about the importance of professional respect, and trusting the experts to show their brilliance and do what they do best. And about not having time to waste on spurious issues, unfounded criticisms, second-guessing that didn't add value. The HR Director could agree with every single objective that Amal put forward, and let him know they were aligned and all wanted to achieve the same outcomes. She took notes and read back every point he made, indicating that they were indeed headed toward the same destination.

Amal nodded, his resolve strengthened by having such a sympathetic partner. "And one more thing," he said. "I want the medicinal chemists to be free of this cross-functional structure and to be in control of each discovery team's agenda." The HR Director knew that would surface, sooner or later in the conversation. And knew this was something the company could never promise, because it would subvert the principle of cross-functional collaboration, which had been the "secret sauce" that was key to the enterprise's game-changing breakthrough success.

Go deep, to Candor. Start where your partner is, the adage says — even if that's a world away from where you want him/her to be. See reality through his or her eyes. Smoke out his/her worries, fears, concerns, needs, desires — and get them on the table, so they can be addressed.

So the HR Director asked Amal to explain why he was intent on hegemony. And what he found difficult, frustrating, distasteful about the Risks that other groups were asking of him, to collaborate and share decision-making and problem-solving authority. Again, Amal didn't let her down. He said it was insulting to be treated like a junior chemist and to have his work critiqued by people who weren't giants in the field. That he'd always been given latitude and autonomy. The more he talked, the more he ramped himself up and got more and more upset.

"I can see how upset you are," the HR Director interjected, when Amal stopped to take a breath. "And I'm sincerely sorry that you're in such a tough situation." She looked like she meant it, with sincere soft eyes, a comforting nod, a lean-forward posture. There was no judgment and no hint of criticism. Negotiating experts call this an "emotional payment." You swallow your pride, connect with your partner on an emotional level and offer something conciliatory to assuage his or her hard feelings. In a way that's sincere, not placating or patronizing.

Again, this emboldened Amal. "I appreciate your support," he said, "but what qualifies you to decide what's a legitimate or out-of-bounds request?" The HR Director felt her face turn red, before she could rein in her indignation. She didn't expect her own credentials to be called into question. But she quickly regained her composure. laughed and reassured Amal that she had the credentials and experience to do her job, as the company's HR Director. She invited him to check her LinkedIn profile, if he wanted to see her CV.

Pivot South, to Risk. Ask a hundred executives where an enabling conversation will take a manager like Amal and they'll all agree. It's going to reinforce his feeling of entitlement, of righteous indignation and keep him comfortably stuck where he is. It will leave him comfortably ensconced in the old paradigm and the old pecking order, where medicinal chemists have hegemony over innovation, with other disciplines following and doing their bidding.

So there's a point in the interaction where the HR Director — or any other coach — needs to change the trajectory, from enabling (which shares Purpose and opens Candor) to ennobling, which asks a fearful, reluctant and put out partner like Amal to lift his game. When driving a car, you avoid collisions and prevent road rage by using a turn signal before you switch from the entrance ramp to the driving lane or from the slow lane into the fast or passing lane. You don't just go. You look for an opening to change lanes and, in tight traffic, catch the eye of the other driver to "let you in."

The same courtesies make it easier to switch lanes in the conversation, from sympathy to ennobling. The HR Director had practiced it many times. She offered a quick affirmation, saying, "I understand how you feel, Amal, and what your objectives are," and quickly following with the question, "Can I ask you some questions, to look at this impasse from another perspective?" As she expected, Amal shifted uneasily, shook his head, and asked whether all of that drawing him out and listening to his perspective was just a set-up or manipulation before letting the other shoe drop. The HR Director kept her composure and assured Amal that she was interested in everything he had to say, and hoped that he'd also be interested in looking at the impasse from someone else's perspective as well, before agreeing on the best path forward. Reluctantly, he acquiesced. The lane change was complete. They were now going to accelerate the conversation and take it in a different, more ennobling, direction.

"What do you think other groups want from you, so they are positioned to make their best contributions?" the HR Director asked. Amal stared at her blankly, then tried to turn the conversation back to his complaints about the way his group had been treated. It wasn't easy to keep him on track and to move him out of his comfort zone, but the HR Director kept at it, and eventually got this begrudging commitment. Amal acknowledged that hegemony is not a birthright to be held and defended by one privileged group, but is thought-leadership that's shared by all groups igniting brilliance and doing their very best to sharpen up each other's thinking and foster innovation. Amal was skeptical. He said he'd give it a try, though he wondered whether biologists, analytical and computational chemists could contribute in more than a support, do-as-we-say role, and wondered whether HR understood enough about the intricacies of drug discovery to weigh in on that debate.

The HR Director leaned forward, with a quizzical look. "I don't get it, Amal," she said. "When you interviewed for this job, we told you about our new paradigm for drug discovery and about the way we have inverted the pyramid. Didn't we explain how and expect all disciplines to step up, innovate and challenge — not just follow orders and do as they are told? You seemed eager, even excited, about being a champion to help us power this forward. What can we rely on from you, to be an active leader, not just a reluctant participant who's going through the motions and acceding to our wishes?"

Amal was stumped, even after the HR Director suggested they should take a break, go back to work and reconvene later in the afternoon. He did offer an apology, unsolicited and unprompted, for his "short order cook" outburst and for "losing it" with the CEO and CTO. And asked if it would be enough to send an apology to them via email, with an explanation why he was pushed to the edge. That was a start, of course. But the HR Director knew that wasn't enough — yet — to lift Amal and the rest of the medicinal chemistry group to the level of participation needed in their respective project teams. And she suggested that he talk with an outside Courage Mentor or leadership coach, to answer the question, "Where do we go from here?"

Look East, to ignite Will. In Hebrew, we call this Activator *hitlahavut*. Literally, it means, lighting a fire within yourself, kindling enthusiasm, getting yourself psyched up and jazzed when you face "the big game," a key presentation, a tough problem or a challenging adversity. Let's leave Amal for a minute and imagine yourself encouraging someone who's deathly afraid of heights and who's got to get down a rope ladder to escape from an unsafe building. "Don't look down. Look me in the eye. IN THE EYE. I'll talk you down this ladder, one rung at a time. Stay with me. We'll get through this together."

How did this work with Amal? He nearly collapsed into his chair when the HR Director brought up the idea of working with an outside coach. Suddenly, the fight went out of him. He went limp, like he'd been punched. Rather than hearing that offer as a vote of confidence and a statement that the company was still willing to invest in his growth, Amal heard it as an indictment. As if he were being sent for remedial tutoring because he wasn't good enough or smart enough. Or because his job was in jeopardy.

Fortunately, the HR Director read the nonverbal cues and responded to the unspoken fear and reluctance. "Amal," she said, "we don't make this resource available to everyone. Only to the CEO, CTO and a few other high-potential members of our team. We have limited money to invest in professional development, and we only spend it where we believe we can get a good return. You are a key member of our team, who's got a lot of potential. We believe in you and need you to step up and seize this opportunity."

Her pep talk wasn't enough to bring a smile back to his face or to get him to lean forward and talk with his usual animated, staccato cadence. But she could see the worry drain out of his face and he asked, "What should I do now, other than waiting for the coach to call?"

Finally, look West for Rigor. Good noble intentions, straight talk, a healthy ego-in-check, insight, self-awareness, good energy. What more could you wish for, to ennoble Amal and equip him to lift his game — so he's an active productive partner in innovation, even if the creative process and its outcomes stretch him beyond his comfort zone, familiarity zone or strike zone?

The answer is "A plan," that includes:

- A mobilization map — which acknowledges and respects the orchestrator's authority to bring the right parties together for the right dialogue and creative process, for pressure-testing and timely solid decisions and for crisp precise-as-a-Swiss-watch execution;

- A situation analysis — pinpointing critical incidents that can become pivot points, to create an inflection point that changes the trajectory and breaks free of the old trendline;

- A program of self-management — that transcends fear and makes Amal a fearful non-retreater who steps up and lifts his head above the parapets rather than a bystander, an avoider or a critical detractor

- A roadmap for idea generation, problem-solving, risk-mitigation and creative improvisation – with Six Sigma, Storyboarding, Future Search or whatever discipline fits the situation;

- A support network — with Sponsors, Advisors, Executors and Co-orchestrators who are mobilized and on belay to support his efforts; and,

- Clear outcomes that measure what matters, that link back to the Primary and Shared Purpose of the improvement effort, and that offer a balanced scorecard that shows progress in engagement, skills, in the loyalty of end-users and Beneficiaries, and in sustainable bottom-line business performance.

Once more, with feeling

We'd love to tell you that you can say the magic words, make the magic motions, ennoble a fearful or reluctant Amal or Sarit to reach new heights and they'll never fall back into their old abyss. You know better. So do we.

Old fears come back, perhaps triggered by new events, by fatigue or by triggers that suddenly inexplicably resurface. And, when that happens, you again may need to start where your partner is, hold him or her on belay, ask the right questions, sympathize, enable, switch lanes and ennoble.

If you're taking Amal aside too often, and talking him down off too many cliffs, that too may be an ennobling conversation — to build his self-soothing reflexes, his ability to regain perspective, and give those who frustrate him more of the benefit of the doubt.

Lifting reluctant and fearful partners from Luddite to luminary

Amal started this journey as a Luddite. He was threatened by the game-changing new way of working that his company pioneered, to the point that he'd rather take a stand and "burn it all down" rather than contribute to its success. Talk about Denial. Did Amal really think he could defend himself and his small elite entourage of medicinal chemists against advances that were designed to make the entire drug discovery process less costly and far more prolific in creating novel, safe, accessible medicines?

Flat matrix structures and upside-down inverted hierarchies can be threatening. They can displace hardworking honest artisans who have worked a lifetime to hone their skills, amass a deep understanding of their craft, earn top credentials and build a following. In the same way that machines threatened the jobs of Luddites, Amal's world was being rocked by high-throughput screening and by computer models that could simulate compounds and analyze their properties and stability before they were synthesized physically on the lab bench. And all of those could tell investors which drug discovery projects should be killed early, because they'd be unlikely to deliver good outcomes.

By 1812, the British Army put down the original Luddites' terrorist attacks and scored a victory for "the wheels of progress." As change accelerated, the high-paid jobs migrated. Engineers and maintenance crews were the new elite, requiring a different skill-set from those who were masters at hand-weaving. In the brave new world that Amal's company was pioneering, the new elites were the trans-disciplinary orchestrators, not the medicinal chemists hand-weaving discrete drug candidates as one-off masterpieces, hoping they would be stable, potent, safe and patentable enough to warrant further investment. It's easy to see why Amal was so threatened and was responding to new ways of working like a 21st Century Luddite when he needed to transform himself into a luminary who could retool and thrive by reshaping his skills, redefining his role and getting into the new game.

Fear is contagious. We see it in negative election campaigns and in the collective madness of an angry mob. The Luddites, like many terrorist groups before and after them, were powered by fear — and fuelled on by threatened short-sighted leaders who played on their fears. How sad that it took an Army rather than an ennobling voice to redirect their energies.

Fortunately, courage is also contagious. You don't have to be a CEO, CTO or HR Director to reach out to someone like Amal, and pull him back from the edge of his fear. As a Project Director, you can get out in front of the sensitivities and start to ennoble before issues come to head, in a public forum, where face-saving can become more compelling than technical or scientific advancement. As a member of the Medicinal Chemistry group, you can show that you revel in the debate and are jazzed when you are invited to improvise with a whole new range of players. As a representative of a foreign culture, you can see when what comes naturally to you is rubbing others the wrong way — and help them adjust to your rhythm and syncopation. Anyone at any level, person-to-person, can read the Purpose, Candor, Risk, Will and Rigor of any matrix, ad hoc, project or virtual team — or of any partner in the team. Anyone can take the 5 Courage Activators, like Amal's HR Director, and can reach out, in person, via phone or email, to ennoble, not just enable. And to lift and activate courage, rather than hoping and waiting for someone "in charge" to take care of it.

Ben Shepherd published a study on PTSD in combat military units. Why, he asked, do some units suffer far fewer cases of battle fatigue, or PTSD, even in the most harrowing of conditions? It's because, he found, they simply didn't allow each other to give in to the fear. They talked to them, coaxed them, joked them, even chided them through the terror and to the other side, saying, as we did to our friend on the ladder, "Look me in the eyes. IN THE EYES. We'll get through this together."

For centuries, we've known about the healing and prophylactic powers of talk. In the best of circumstances, when we know we are preparing for a personal or family struggle, we reach out, ennoble and encourage one another. In oppressive conditions, POW camps and slave trades, captors take away those uplifting connections, knowing that one person's strength can embolden someone else. The choice — whether to be a captor or an encourager — does not reside in the Board Room or CEO's office. It's yours alone to make, wherever you sit in the organization.

The hardest Luddites to work with are not those, like Amal, who make their reservations known and declare their fear. It's the Impostors, the ones who say all the right things, who "talk the talk" of Purpose, Candor and Risk. Who fake the Will. And who then hide in the matrix, heads down below the parapets, who stonewall in response to emails and action items, accidently-on-Purpose drop the ball, mutter a cynical or courage-eroding comment when a good noise and affirmation would be more helpful. These are the Imposters, says retired Orion Capital CEO and University of Hartford Business Professor Larry Hollen, who oversaw the transformation of his workers compensation insurance company into the most profitable enterprise in his industry by inverting the innovation pyramid and asking Loss Control and Case Management to show up in the driver's seat rather than in a behind-the-scenes support role.

You can coach Luddites, Hollen says, as long as they are willing to look beyond their fear and ignite their own — and others' brilliance. But Imposters are different. They hold onto their fear, reluctance, entitlements like a badge of honor. They may build a bunker and fortress to protect their interests and divert time, energy, resources and courage by simply waiting you out and wearing you down. Imposters, Hollen says, have to be moved aside, where they cannot divert bandwidth or resources, deflate or thwart initiative. They need a zero tolerance policy, imposed not just by those in charge — but by anyone who's felt their betrayal or duplicity or watched them betray someone close to them . And that courage, too, is contagious.

Chapter 8
Start Up Nation:
How Israel Encodes Brilliance into Its DNA

Brainstorming has strict rules. No criticism, no nay-saying, lots of encouragement to think out-of-the-box, go wild and crazy, follow your imagination wherever it takes you. In a mental sprint, rather than a marathon, a group is supposed to dream up as many ideas as possible for whatever opportunity it is trying to seize or whatever problem it is trying to solve. Brainstorming is supposed to establish a safe environment for creativity, throwing off the chains of scrutiny and critical thinking. When no one has to worry about whether a weird idea will seem silly, outrageous or politically offensive, innovation is supposed to flourish.

Providing a safe place for original, even deviant, thinking sounds good in theory. Research attests to the benefits. An environment free of criticism and challenges feels good. Participants enjoy blue-sky sessions that give them kudos and gold stars for their bright ideas. They walk away charged up and affirmed. But, despite the good will it generates, there is little research to support the theory that brainstorming actually produces more ideas, better ideas or that it actually accelerates innovation (Lehrer, 2012). In fact, the protective bubble of all-positive, no-debate, nothing-to-fear dialogue may actually inhibit Candor, Rigor, and Risk, in its zeal to protect Will. Which inevitably erodes Purpose.

Watch a typical Israeli team grapple with a vexing problem. The activity you'll see is about as far away from brainstorming as you can get. If eight colleagues huddle in a conference room, there are at least four different conversations going on at once, with people shouting over each other, gesturing for attention, pointing to direct traffic, banging on the table if that's what it takes to be heard. Communication experts call it a synchronous (rather than a sequential) conversation style. It can be daunting and overwhelming to Americans and other Anglophones, who are used to a rhythm where each speaker takes a turn and waits for a pause to get permission to speak. It looks chaotic, even ill-mannered, if you don't know how to decode the interaction. If you try to get up to speed up, merge and enter the traffic flow with Anglophone manners, you'll find yourself shut out. And, if you're a CEO or Professor-credentialed thought-leader, who's used to deference when you say, "Here's what we should do. Follow me," it can seem downright disrespectful or even insubordinate to have your judgments challenged.

Dynamic tension

Any junior high school chemistry student can tell you which compounds to mix to create an exothermic reaction — because those two materials, when thrown together, create heat. The same is true when you bring together certain diverse personalities or cross-functional perspectives, give them a problem, add oxygen and stir.

Turning up the heat is something that Dr Oren Becker expects when he puts together a cross-functional team at his pharmaceutical company,

Dynamix. Becker is clear on what conflict should do. The point isn't for one discipline to "win," by neutralizing the opposition, overcoming objections, addressing concerns and getting their way. It's for each team member to push, probe, pressure-test and spark an even higher level of ingenuity and creativity, to improve the total team's output.

Becker knows that computational and medicinal chemists see things differently. And that biologists have an even different perspective. As do the finance, patent and IT functions. When Becker hires large, he's not just looking for the best thinkers in a particular discipline. That's simply not enough. He's also looking for people who have egos that will withstand the push-and-pull and can work transparently, knowing that someone else will flag things that they've overlooked – or that are sub-optimal. Or who can quickly ramp themselves up, get their egos under control and get with the program of living with dynamic tension.

In our first book on courage (Klein and Napier, 2003), we warned that teams today face conflict-prone realities and can't master those realities with conflict-avoidant norms. Instead, we need the courage to face tough issues head-on, even when they make us uncomfortable or threaten our time-tested assumptions about how things work. We need the courage to invite people to the table, knowing full well that they may present contrarian perspectives and may oppose the very proposals that we are most passionate about championing and taking forward.

Our first executive coaching client in Israel was a polite genteel engineer from Alabama USA, given an expat assignment as the Managing Director of a new start-up telecom venture in Israel. He was a Southern gentleman who dressed impeccably, spoke quietly and listened intently. By the time we met, he was at his wit's end. "Who can solve problems in an environment of shouting, finger-pointing, name-calling and noise?" he asked, half-expectantly and half-rhetorically. "Tell me. How can I turn down the heat, when we've got a tough engineering or planning issue to tackle?" he said.

Turn *down* the heat? Sure, that would make things more comfortable for a methodical, orderly Southern gentleman. But was that *really* what this team needed, to overcome formidable engineering challenges quickly and capital-efficiently — and have the infrastructure ready for a smooth flawless product launch?

We invited our friend from Alabama to take a deeper look at the tension and assess the team's **Will** to succeed and overcome the adversities they faced. What did he see? No one in the team was stifled or beaten down by the dynamic tension in the room. Instead, they were called to attention, sharpened, energized by the taunting and name-calling, the raised voices and waving hands, by someone going up to the white board, drawing a red X through someone else's sketches and drawing their own ideas in the margins. At the end of what looked like a knock-down, drag-out raucous skull-session, with interrupts and raised voices on highly contentious issues, everyone walked out of the conference room with big smiles, slapping each other on the back like Rugby players who've just scored a goal, and have taken a few bumps and bruises along the way. And with an elegant solution to what looked like an insurmountable problem — to increase bandwidth and prevent dropped calls, without having to invest millions of dollars building new towers.

So what does this mean for you — if you aren't the CEO and Founder or the Managing Director? Suppose you're the Project Manager or the head of a Finance, Engineering, Marketing or Quality function who's pushing forward the next game-changing innovation? How do you encode dynamic tension into the DNA of a team that might be wired more like our friend from Alabama — or that gets gridlocked by factions trying to score points at one another's expense, rather than coming together to pool know-how and solve vexing problems? Follow the roadmap through the 5 Activators:

- **Rigor.** Identify the key issues that need to be tackled, so you can orchestrate the right debate and figure out how, when and where to bring together divergent perspectives. That allows you to flatten the power hierarchy and stir the pot to create an exothermic reaction. Bring people together who will disagree. Who may not get along. And invite dissent.

- **Purpose.** Instead of throwing people with diverse perspectives into a room and hoping for the best, articulate common ground and mutual interests. Provide clear criteria to cull through brainstormed ideas and keep working the problem until all of the success criteria are satisfied. These apply whether you need a way to deliver service that redefines the trendline and generates more than a small incremental boost in profits. Or you need to create a better, safer and more economically accessible health solution. Or a more environmentally friendly fuel.

- **Risk.** Establish a code of honor to hold in check parochial ambitions and professional egos and keep them subservient to the Purpose that you've brought the group together to achieve. Get to a few key individuals off-line, before your videoconference or team meeting,

163

especially if they need a few pointers to show up ready to attack issues, rather than people, and bridge cross-cultural or personality differences effectively. Depoliticize debates, so victory isn't "neutralizing the opposition and getting support for my faction's position," but for seizing the right opportunities and overcoming obstacles that could diminish enterprise-success.

- **Candor.** If you think that robust debate and a healthy exchange of ideas begins when your team enters the meeting room or dials in to a video conference, think again. Use online sharing to bring the parties together virtually — and to frame issues, exchange ideas and make sure your participants understand the technical and business context. Provide an executive summary for the time-pressured and big-picture thinkers, and detail for those who wish to dig deeper. Ask questions, so you know what people think (and how they think) before the real action and interaction begins.

- **Will.** Our friend from Alabama inherited a mature team in Israel. A team that already knew how to assess each other's level of emotional engagement, and pull in key thought-leaders who were sitting on the sidelines as bystanders. And could lift each other's spirits, without shepherding and facilitation from the "official" team leader. Your team may not be this mature. They may need you, as the orchestrator, to get under their wings and give them lift, when you notice they're stuck, inhibited or fatigued. Or find an outside facilitator who can play this role for you, and then teach the group to do it for themselves.

Elephant skin, happiness and the joy of dissatisfaction

The give-and-take sparring that characterizes Israeli teams seems to be a male sport. Especially when it helps to have a booming voice that can be heard above the din. So we asked Ruti Alon, General Partner at venture capital firm Pitango, whether this kind of give-and-take is something that puts women business leaders at a disadvantage. If anyone would have the perspective to answer this, it was Ruti, whose position as Chairperson and the driving force behind the establishment of the Israeli Life Sciences Industry (ILSI) trade association gives her a broad view of people and trends within the industry.

Ruti dismissed the question as "shtui'ot" (nonsense). She does not think there is a gender gap or a glass ceiling in Israel. Nor does she think women, as a group, have any more or less courage to debate, wrestle down the real issues, and do it with zeal and passion, than men. As Ruti spoke further and elaborated on the toughness it takes to hold your own in an Israeli business or scientific collaboration, and the elephant skin you need to not take it personally when your assumptions and biases are questioned, she sounded like Tom Hanks' character, Jimmy Dugan, manager of the Rockford Peaches in the All-Girls American Professional Baseball League, who proclaimed, "There is no crying [allowed] in baseball."

Ruti explained that the life sciences – even more than any other high-tech field – is a tough business where there are very few easy solutions. You've got to probe, challenge, get deep knowledge of your domain and elicit the very best thinking you can from every single member of the team. It's not personal. The slightest deviation on the bench can invalidate your experiment and the slightest lack of Rigor with a patient can compromise your chances of success in the clinic.

If you're the orchestrator bringing diverse perspectives together to create new and complex discoveries, you've got to find a way to get your voice heard, whether you're asking questions that haven't yet been answered or putting forward ideas that can create a breakthrough. If you are soft-spoken, you have to find a way to lower the volume, without inhibiting the team's spirit, so you can be heard above the din. If it takes you a while to get to the point and you're working with an impatient group, you may have to rehearse off-line, so you can enter the discussion with a few attention-getting zingers. You may need to learn to talk with your hands and your facial expressions, as well as your words. And make your presence felt. Or, if all else fails, you may need to enlist someone else's help to open the door for you and get you the hearing you need — or present your case, as your proxy. Based on her experience, Ruti believes that women can do this just as well as men.

Happiness may well be the key to the high level of brilliance, innovation and productive dynamic tension in Israel. It seems counter-intuitive, in a country that's always under threat of attack, that's still officially "at war" with a few of its neighbors, that has very few natural resources and very little manufacturing base to shore up its economy. Yet, happiness surveys show that Israel has the third-highest youth happiness index in the world, a low suicide rate, low incidence of PTSD and other emotional scars of war among its military. Gallup polls say that Israelis rate seventh in the world on the "happiness index," well ahead of societies like the US and UK.

Elephant skin. That's what Israelis call the toughness to take criticism, naysaying, even personal ridicule on board, without allowing negativity or opposition to deflate their Will.   Mood gives people the resilience to bounce back from criticism with an indefatigable optimism. So, if we want to toughen people up, the best way to do it is to get them to laugh, to celebrate success, to lift their spirits.

Instinctively, we know this. As parents and grandparents, aunts and uncles, we know to smile, tease and tickle our toddler children before changing their diapers or getting them to try a vegetable that tastes weird. We remember how Mark Twain's fictional character, Huck Finn, enlisted the help of others to paint the fence — by pretending it was great fun so convincingly that it actually *made* the activity a joy.   "Women have a different way of generating this uplifting spirit than men," Ruti told us. Women may have a different vocal range, rhythm, timbre than men, she said, and they may learn to lead by playing support and technical roles rather than combat roles in the Army, but that doesn't mean that a softer or higher-pitched voice can't or won't be heard — unless a woman chooses to give up or be stifled, or unless she can't show that her perspective really does add value and contribute to breakthrough solutions.

Israel's President Shimon Peres, at age 90, describes the secret sauce in the Israeli DNA as the joy of dissatisfaction. He says that dissatisfaction is a key part of the Jewish character. Dissatisfaction is what creates the burning desire to probe deeper and push the outer edges of scientific discovery. It's why so many Nobel prize winners, so many patents and so many game-changing scientific breakthroughs that have come out of such a small tribe. Give some people an insurmountable problem and they'll find a way to surrender and make peace with the situation. Give Israelis a situation that's already 70% or 80% good, and they'll focus on the 20-30% that can be improved.

Joy isn't about frivolity, happiness expert Tal ben Shachar tells us. It's about finding pleasure in the little things, the victories we create, the achievements we accomplish, the problems we solve, the brilliant discoveries that open the door to new possibilities. Which brings us back to Dr Oren Becker and the dynamic tension he infuses in science and business development teams at Dynamix. There are times that team leaders seem overwhelmed and daunted, almost on the verge of tears. They turn to Becker for the answers, since he's the world-class expert, the CEO, CTO, the master Professor. More than once, we've seen Becker smile, reassure an anxious protégé and politely refuse to solve technical problems for them, reminding his team leads how good *they* are, how much he relies on *them,* and how much he looks forward to *their* ideas. He refuses to lower the standards or compromise the goals. Or back off when there are problems to put right. And he does it all with a radiant smile, a grace, an expression of confidence and, most of all, a heartfelt celebration of success when milestones — even small milestones — are achieved. Joy. Who'd have thought it's what toughens people up.

Adversity and triumph

At age 18, a young woman was selected by the Israeli Army for Medical Corps Training. Since she'd struggled to earn good math and science grades in high school, the placement came as a surprise — but her photographic memory, her ability to see graphics and drawings in three dimensions and her nerves of steel were flagged in the Army placement tests. So off she went for six months of rigorous EMT training, as an ambulance aide by day and a cram-course student of anatomy, nursing, biochemistry and medical ethics at night.

After 16 months of training and fieldwork, before her 20th birthday, our friends' daughter was running training simulations for surgeons returning to the Army for reserve duty. She described her role, as a young woman and rookie paramedic, training experienced, strong-willed, 40-year-old male surgeons. "It's not my job to teach them surgical or medical techniques," she said, realizing that she'd have no credibility if she overstepped and tried to show off any of her new medical knowledge. "But it is my job to get them to critique each other, and to create conditions that will simulate the adversities they might face, if G-d forbid, we face a real threat." In other words, to Power Up their Brilliance — and unlock their power to come up with the best, not necessarily the easiest or obvious, answers.

By age 20, our friends' daughter learned valuable lessons about Powering Up Brilliance in teams — how to pinpoint the real issues and create the right dynamic tension among bona-fide experts who were far more experienced, far more successful and far more dominant personalities. And how to use her femininity, her unique cultural background as the daughter of Anglo/American immigrants, her presence and charm — not power, position or authority — to orchestrate the right debates. And to depoliticize the debate, so good rational decision-making could prevail. Her greatest joy came when the Israeli Army field surgeons were highlighted on their rescue mission in Haiti, following the devastating earthquake. "Those are my guys," she said with pride, "and look at what they're doing. That's what they learned to do on my watch!"

This is the epitome of what Ruti meant when she said, "Gender isn't the issue." And said that there's no glass ceiling for women who own their power, wrestle the tough issues, show their competence and command respect — in a way that works for them.

There's no doubt that our friends' daughter is an outlier. But, in many respects, her Army experience is no different from that of most Israeli youths with an aptitude for leadership and for brilliant scientific or technical problem-solving. While American and Canadian, British, Australian and New Zealand youth are packing up and heading to university, Israeli youth of the same age head to the Army or National Service, or both. While young adults in these English-speaking countries get a reprieve from real-world responsibility while they fill their heads with knowledge and broaden their perspectives, Israeli youth are assuming the mantle of leadership with jobs that have real life-or-death consequences.

What's more, the Israeli Army, like many matrix organizations in the corporate world, is a flat enterprise. By age 21 or 22, it's not unusual to find a junior officer in a field position that requires him/her to make a decision or solve a problem — now — not radio to headquarters to describe the situation and wait for someone at a higher level to make a decision and give them marching orders.

Make no mistake. Even in a book with insights on courage, we aren't making a political statement about military service. Nor are we saying that all countries should mobilize as if they are under siege and on constant alert, like we are in Israel. Even in Israel, most parents would give almost anything to achieve a state of peace that made it unnecessary for their children (and grandchildren) to serve.

What we *are* saying is that there's something encoded in the DNA of the culture that tells Israelis — in their youngest and most formative stages of career — not to expect things to be easy, secure, simple, predictable. To accept adversity and take it in stride, as a fact of life. To feel spurred to action, rather than betrayed, by the fact that there is no comfort zone, no secure career path or predictable guaranteed career ladder. To take joy in what you're able to accomplish. To realize that even if "you built it," you didn't do it alone but with help from people who believe and invest in your success.

Existential threats, in the world outside Israel, may not require other countries to mobilize for universal Army service. But there may be something worth emulating in the way that we condition ourselves and our next generation to face adversity. To look at the loss of a job as an inevitable transition that will happen two, three or more times in a career — rather than viewing those who are in transition as "casualties" and those who are retained as "survivors." To realize that someone can disagree vehemently in a meeting and that doesn't mean they are "shooting you in the back" if they find flaws in your proposals. To fail fast when we embark on a new technology or new investment — so we can move on to something else that is more worthwhile, in a way that earns the confidence of our investors and board members, without worry about "keeping this particular enterprise alive." Not to expect things to do be easy, secure, comfortable, predictable and set up for guaranteed success, as long as you follow orders and tick the blocks on your project plan. And, through it all, to keep smiling

The Intel Israel experience

More than a decade after Gulf War I, Dov Frohman published a book about the success of Intel Israel when Tel Aviv was under rocket fire from Saddam Hussein. His titled his book, *Leadership the Hard Way*. Like every other story about the Israeli innovation ecosystem, his is not a story about fear and desperation. Nor is it a story about grinding it out, day after day, stressed and overworked. It is a story about triumph over adversity, pulling together and initiative — with pride and joy.

With rockets falling on Tel Aviv, Homeland Defense declared a national emergency. Schools were closed. Businesses that were not certified as critical for national security were ordered to cease operation. In his book, Frohman explains his counter-intuitive logic. "If we had complied with the security directives, no one at Intel HQ would have criticized us. They would have been sympathetic. But, to be responsible to the shareholders, they would have called an emergency board meeting and insisted on moving enterprise-critical assets out of Israel. Which is exactly the victory that Saddam Hussein wanted."

So, instead of complying with the security directive, Frohman called his MEC together, explained the consequences of compliance, and asked, "How can we keep Intel Israel open for business so we deliver engineering and products on time and budget, as if it were "business as usual?"

Think of it. Does this seem reasonable and responsible to you? Should a key executive like Frohman, responsible for nearly 10,000 employees, to declare, "Business as usual," and insist that the enterprise stay open, when Homeland Defense is saying, "Stay home and stay under cover?" And to lift, rather than suspend, their standards at when employees are concerned about the safety of their families and communities more than their projects and product pipelines?

In the mid-1980s, at the start of the big technology boom in the USA, psychiatrist Judith Bardwick published her seminal book, Danger in the Comfort Zone (2nd edition, 1995), which warned about the downsides of a business culture that rewards effort rather than results, promises easy and secure career paths, fosters entitlement and treats average performance as if it merits gold stars. The easy path may feel good, she acknowledged, but it simply isn't sustainable. What's worse, it leaves people feeling betrayed and less able to cope when adversity does hit, when the bar is raised and what used to be "good enough" is no longer enough to meet regulatory or competitive requirements.

Bardwick described the backlash that leaders face when they deliver the harsh news that entitlements, career paths, protected positions and generously lax performance standards are not sustainable – and say, like Dr C, "March or die." Her caveat: Don't be surprised when your call to action evokes fear among late adopters who think you're being unkind, ungenerous, overly demanding, hypercritical or who accuse you of arbitrarily reneging on old promises. Her prescription: Courage, to take the heat, stand your ground, explain the rationale behind new standards and new formulas for compensation and job security, and rely on early adopters to help allay fear, raise confidence and bring around late adopters.

Bardwick's analysis of what she called "the entitlement trap" focused on American businesses. But what happens in a society, like Israel, where people have different expectations? Where what's expected is more akin to a pioneering spirit rather than a "job for life?" Or an understanding that success requires you to add value rather than keep your head down, do as you're told and not make waves? As new immigrants from English-speaking countries complain about the adversities of life in Israel, veterans reply, "So? What do you expect? You're building a country. This is Israel. Buck up. Get with the program."

In *Leadership the Hard Way*, Frohman describes the mobilization that occurred as his call to action took hold. How quick action got Intel Israel reclassified as an enterprise that's essential to National Security, because of its economic impact, its prominence on the world high-tech stage and the number of jobs at stake. How they built daycare centers, arranged for alternative transportation and housing, set up secure internet and telephone connections to enable working remotely, even from shelters if necessary. And did all this with determination, with smiles, with encouragement, in addition to doing their "day jobs," which, in normal circumstances, were already intense and demanding.

Todd Dollinger and Steve Rhodes, co-founders and principals of The Trendlines Group, a management and investment company that runs two high-tech business incubators in Israel, say that Israel isn't just a Start Up hotbed. More than that, they observe, the entire country is a start-up, an experiment, a new venture that began in the late 1800s, when Jews started to seek freedom and independence by moving back to their historical homeland and reclaiming their roots. Each successive wave of immigration — from Western Europe and the Arabian Peninsula, from North Africa and South America, from Ethiopia and the former USSR — has brought new pressures to the country, along with new skill-sets and new opportunities. And a zeal for "just being here," which is palpable for anyone who walks through the gates and exits the Customs Hall at Ben Gurion airport.

In this kind of culture, it's no wonder that Frohman would get a mobilization rather than "the-old-man-is-crazy" response when he called his Intel team to action and said, "We can't roll over and take this lying down." And it's no wonder that there's a willingness to experiment, to fail forward — quickly and inexpensively — and to regroup, bounce back and learn from the experience, so a failed business venture does not become a career red-liner.

Possibility thinking, a can-do, take-charge of the future mentality is part of the DNA in Israel, among Arabs as well as Jews. The question isn't "Why isn't this possible?" It's "What are the obstacles?" and "How can we invent something new and improvise to overcome them?" It isn't, "Who's to blame?" But, "Who can I rely on?" It isn't, "Whose permission do I need?" but, "What initiative can I take?"

Innovation expert Janet Sarnack (2012) calls this generative thinking, creating "mind-flips" to turn impossibility and adversity into breakthrough opportunity. It starts with what positive psychology guru Martin Seligman (1998) calls "a healthy defense against reality which creates optimism by looking at 'what can be' rather than 'what is' and 'what has been.'" With blue-sky questions that begin adaptive inquiry. And with an active, rather than a passive or fatalist, role to create luck rather than settle for what fate has in store. Whether or not you live in Israel — or have visited or led a collaboration here   this is a dialogue you can spark with Purpose, Candor, Will, Rigor and Risk. To create your own economic miracles.

Is it sustainable?

Who knows if the so-called "Israeli economic miracle" is sustainable. Time will tell. Economic architects like Professor Stanley Fischer, an immigrant from Zambia who was appointed Governor of the Bank of Israel, looks ahead with caution. The whole powerhouse may unravel, he warns, without massive investments in education, to produce a next generation of talent like the one that is aging. Without austerity measures, to convert welfare recipients and unionized government workers into a workforce that contributes to the GDP rather than living off the largess of the State. And without a next wave of change that will take the country from being a high-tech source of innovation to a partnership and enterprise-growing hub (Staub, 2010).

We'll see whether the country and its leaders will have the courage to take warnings from Professor Fischer and others to heart --- and sustain the success that has already been achieved. But, for now, the economic miracle is impressive. By almost any success metric, the country is thriving. So much, that it's been called the StartUp Nation (Senor and Singer, 2009), the ImagineNation (Sernack, 2012) and has been heralded for Changing the

World through Innovation (Davis, 2005), for being in a class by itself in the Israel Test (Gilder & Lieberman, 2012). Success is reflected in new job growth, an influx of R&D investments, entrepreneurial ventures, and global economic expansion of Israeli ventures. All this, in a country that functions as an island, bordered by an ocean on the West and un-crossable borders to the North, East and South; that has few natural resources including a shortage of water; that is perpetually on guard and under threat or attack.

And that revels in overcoming these adversities and making lemonade out of lemons.

"Come to the edge," he said.

They said, "We are afraid."

"Come to the edge," he said.

"We might fall," they said.

"COME TO THE EDGE," he said.

And they came. And he pushed. And they flew.

   - A poem by Guilliame Apollinaire

Chapter 9
Coach: Three Faces with the Power of Tough Love

You can tell a lot about someone from the people who surround them, the kind of offices they keep, how they look at you, what hangs on their wall, how they dress, how they talk to the staff. As you wait to be ushered in for an appointment, it all forms a quick snapshot. It's a moment, frozen in time that reveals everything, including how much someone wishes to reveal or keep hidden.

That's true when you're interviewing for a job and trying to size up how it would be to work here, with the people interviewing as colleagues, and a few as your immediate or matrix-structure supervisors. It's true when you're doing an inspection or due diligence for an investor, potential development partner or regulator. When, like us, you're there to assess the capabilities of an organization or a team and its leaders. Or when you're there, as a writer, to chronicle someone's achievements and the Brilliance they've Powered Up in others.

This chapter includes three very different snapshots — one, a posh biotech office in Ramat Gan, in the Tel Aviv metropolis; second, a basement office in Temple University's basketball complex in North Philadelphia; and, third, the mobile phone, laptop and makeshift huddle spaces commandeered by a road warrior with an international corporation.

The snapshot at the Ramat Gan office tower

Elegance, grace, style. From the artwork, awards and photos that were thoughtfully arranged in the reception area to the colors of the walls and the tasteful, functional but definitely not opulent furnishings, it was clear that the space had been well planned and designed. As soon as we met the senior founder of the company, Dr Silvi Noiman, we could see where the style and panache originated. Dr Noiman was as elegant as her surroundings and greeted us with a warm smile.

The receptionist had told us, "Dr Noiman is expecting you." It didn't take us long to see how true that was. Sitting on the table were a fresh cappuccino and a cup of English tea, along with a plate of fruit. Dr Noiman had done her homework and already anticipated what we'd want to drink. She was a gracious and welcoming host.

At least a dozen young people were huddled in their offices, talking in clusters of 3-4 at a desk. By Israeli standards, they were dressed up. A few of the young men — team leads, we learned later — wore ties. The young women in leadership roles were dressed like Dr Noiman — in elegant pants suits, with tailored blazers and a dash of color. There were no T-shirts, tank tops or open-toe sandals, not even among the technicians.

In the hallways and public areas, voices were hushed, like a library or the quiet car of a train. There was no shouting down the hallway and no overpowering voices. Despite the lack of noise, you could feel the "buzz" in every part of the office. People had a bounce in their step and a sense of urgency and excitement about their discoveries. They were turned on and jazzed about their projects, excited about being on the cutting edge, and took as much pride in their powerpoints and spreadsheets as in the spotlessness of their surroundings.

We weren't surprised when Dr Noiman talked about excellence, about attention to detail, and about the importance of anticipating down-the-road consequences. "We're making drugs, not software," she said, in a tone that established a common ground and didn't sound a bit condescending, even though it was pretty basic for consultants who were life sciences specialists, "We want people to be innovative, but to understand that it all has to be 100% perfect when it leaves our office. That's why pride, excellence and care are so important — and why I press people to make sure they're up on the latest journals and the latest standards, and double-check to make sure nothing leaves this office that we can't be proud to call 'ours.'"

In that first meeting in Dr Noiman's office, we could tell that she was evaluating us. She was careful with what she revealed about her management practices, her leadership philosophy, her concerns about the way the enterprise she had founded was scaling up, now that she was sharing power with a CEO in Boston and a Chief Technical Officer (CTO) alongside her in Ramat Gan. Her probes were as careful and precise as her answers, when she asked about our backgrounds and about why her board and CEO were making an investment in something as murky as "leadership development." She was too polite to challenge us directly, but we could see she was skeptical.

It took several months for Dr Noiman to trust us with "her" people and believe that we could contribute to their success in a meaningful way. Not that there was ever a sharp or disrespectful word in the interim. But we

181

could tell when we crossed the threshold. Almost overnight, she raised her standards. Quickened the pace. Sharpened the repartee. Demanded practical, not just philosophical, answers to leadership dilemmas — and demanded to see quick improvements in the way that her leads were handling tough cross-cultural situations. After we crossed the threshold, every hour with Dr Noiman was an intense mental work-out that left us fulfilled and proud about what we'd delivered to her and her colleagues, when we walked across the bridge into Tel Aviv and boarded the train to return our home in the Northern Galilee. And tired.

Which is what Dr Noiman's team members told us that they also experienced, wrestling down scientific issues, building new software and new computer models, guiding and challenging their colleagues from other scientific and business disciplines in other locations. We never heard Dr Noiman say anything overtly critical to any of "her" people in public. But we heard lots of challenging questions like, "Have you read the latest journal articles on this mechanism of action?" or "When will this be ready?" or "Can I be sure this is excellent enough to present it to the board" or "How have you changed your recommendations to the chemistry team, based on the latest research at last week's medical conference?" Israeli officers are expected to lead from the front and take their troops into dangerous maneuvers saying, *"Acharei!"* (after me!). When it came to taking a scientific team to new heights of discovery and innovation, with a sense of urgency and an eye on the prize, Dr Noiman also led from the front.

In private conversations and public praise, Dr Noiman told us what each key member of her team was capable of contributing — and how she had a "sixth sense" to see their real potential, sometimes before they saw it in themselves. "I know what you can do," she'd say, beaming with a pride smile, "and know you won't let us down." She'd phone, out of the blue, to alert us about a problem that was brewing, so we'd be focused and prepared to give it our best thought — just as she did with her scientific leaders and her finance and bookkeeping staff. Surveys confirmed what we all felt — her loyalty, her belief in us, her insistence that we not let anyone on the team down in any way, no matter how hard we had to push ourselves.

Rigor was the most visible of the 5 Activators when we first met Dr Noiman and set foot in her offices. From the spotless counters in the lunch area to the pictures on the wall, the letter-perfect reports, her insistence on more than pedestrian conventional tried-and-true discoveries to produce out-of-the-box breakthroughs and groundbreaking discoveries, and a photographic memory about where, exactly, a particular research result was published or who had what molecule on patent — and the long hours of probing, deliberation and care to deliver what she called "excellence." But Dr Noiman's magic wasn't in the Rigor per se. It was the way she built the foundation, so Rigor came "from the heart" and was born of pride and accomplishment, rather than fear.

Risk was the Activator that members of Dr Noiman's team still describe, when they talk about working with her. They are acutely aware of the trust that she placed in them and appreciative of the time and care she devoted to coaching them and developing their potential. They knew she was only a phone call away, no matter where she was travelling and what other obligations she had. They could count on her for hands-on support and guidance when they were given stretch goals, rather than being thrown into a daunting assignment and being told to "sink or swim." Over and over again people told us how deeply Dr Noiman cared about them, understood their career aspirations and family obligations, checked in to ask, "How's it going?" and "How are you feeling." And listened. Paying attention to details — and delivering excellence — wasn't just a matter of "pleasing the boss," it was a way of honoring the trust that Dr Noiman had placed in them and showing the same loyalty to her and to the team that they had been shown.

Candor, or, as Dr Noiman called it, "transparency," was not just a Activator that she practiced; it was a core value instilled into the DNA of the company. No one worked in isolation; peer review was not just encouraged, but expected. Every report, result, experiment was posted where it would be visible. Every plan and update was challenged, to see how progress could be accelerated. In meetings, project reviews, idea exchanges, she asked probing questions, named "the elephants in the room," and deputized team leads to create an environment of open debate, wrestling down key issues, challenging assumptions, all in the name of making things better. And, in her patented "take you under her wing and coach you" style, she'd spot the people who were put off, defensive, threatened by that kind of transparency — or who felt their professional credentials or rank in the company should make them immune from being asked tough questions. And would give them the care and attention they needed to shed the armor of defensiveness and engage in a robust and open idea-exchange.

Will. With high standards, a fast pace and peer review, there's bound to be residual heat — in the form of frustration, bruised egos, fatigue. Rather

184

than reducing the pressure for excellence or stifling peer review and healthy debate, Dr Noiman lifted the energy, confidence and resolve of teammates who were "having a bad day" or felt bruised by the process. "Yes you can," was her message. "I see your potential. You've got the right stuff. This is your job and I'm behind you to make the stretch." And she knew exactly how to tailor that message to each individual — with humor or seriousness, with toughness or a gentle touch, and with the right mix of "I'm-here-for-support" or "Do-it-on-your-own." She'd switch fluently between Spanish, Hebrew and English. As a result, she got people to play above their game, with pride and joy in what they were able to accomplish.

Purpose had three aspects — to advance medical science and battle against human disease, to grow a successful company dedicated to excellence, and to do it in a way that shows the best of the best of Israeli leadership. Science/medicine, business growth, national pride. For those who were part of Dr Noiman's inner circle, it was never about "me" or about "ego." And never about personal profit or greed. She had no problem explaining *why* she counted on team members to transcend fear, reluctance, frustration, convenience — and do what is right, excellent, what will make everyone proud instead. And walked that talk herself.

The snapshot at the North Philadelphia basketball complex

It's been a long time since we visited John Chaney in his basement office at Temple University. It's over a decade since he announced his retirement. But the snapshot still is clear. We noticed three things when we entered Coach's space. First, of course, were the basketball players milling around

— talking easily, laughing, a trickling stream of young energetic men and women sprinkled with a few coaches and management types, all flowing through a contained space. Second, were Coach's mottoes, hanging on bold banners that said, BE THE DREAM, DIAMONDS COME FROM PRESSURE and WINNING IS AN ATTITUDE. Third was Besse, a den mother if there ever was one, sweet talking the crowd, checking in with folks, bringing some kind of order to the chaos and activity going on. Besse had been part of Temple University for more than 30 years, well before John Chaney joined her and breathed new life into Temple basketball, well before he made winning an attitude.

Coach Chaney was a little late for our interview. He apologized, never mentioning that he had been with a friend who had been diagnosed with cancer, and it was up to John to provide hope, to lift him up and get him to muster the courage to transcend the blow that fate had dealt him, as John does with everyone. When you sit down with Coach, you see that he looks nothing like the wild-eyed owl-faced sorcerer who was portrayed on national television. On the court and certainly on national TV, Coach looked bigger than life — arms waving, shouting at the referees, goading his own players, a man possessed, a tad shy of being a certifiable maniac. In his day, he was a compelling figure in his rumpled white dress shirt, sleeves rolled up, eyes blazing, leaping up to defend his players or throw some advice that they should take to heart — now.

But, here in the office, we saw a different Coach. Loose. Thoughtful. A master at looking into the souls of human beings, looking past the bravado and the press releases and scouting reports and sizing up their potential, long before they have the brilliance to actually "be the dream" rather than wishing it would magically just come true.

Coach Chaney's door is open for anyone who manages to get by Besse. Many times during our two-hour visit, a face appeared at the door. Besse said, "He'll be glad to see you." And he was. Coach stopped in midsentence, got up, introduced the person with great pride and offered some outrageous, heart-felt compliment or an affectionate aside with enough truth to be believed. He was like a loving father welcoming a child who had been away for a long time even though it might have been only a few days. The brief interchange started and ended with a big hug, always with sincerity, never a throwaway.

Within seconds, we were struck by how well Coach Chaney knew each of his visitors. What he knew wasn't just their achievements on the basketball court, their athletic prowess, or the raw talent and potential that made Chaney and his coaching staff want to recruit them for Temple in the first place. Of course, he knew all that and could recall specific incidents in specific games where each player had exhibited the very best of his athletic potential.

But Coach Chaney knew far more. He knew each player's dreams, ambitions and the fears and self-doubts that could trip them up and erase their courage to act. He understood the temptations that could tip the scales and the fine line between being successful and being a college basketball has-been, between doing your family proud and letting them down. He understood that it wasn't just their own dreams and ambitions that each of these young athletes carried into Temple and beyond with them, but the hopes and dreams of single mothers and extended families who had sacrificed dearly to give these young men a shot at a better life.

The first visitor to appear at the door was Greg, newly arrived from Jacksonville, a tall freshman, perhaps 6' 7" (2 meters), who was taking the toughest course-load he could image — pre-engineering. When he appeared, Coach leaped up, hugged him and talked about his size eighteen shoes, wondering just how big he would get. That introduction passed on to news about his mother and sister and then how he was getting along on campus. Then there was a word about being sure to hang out with the kids who were good for him.

In only a few clipped sentences, Coach succeeded in providing lots of warmth, recognition, support. The season didn't begin for another month, but Coach Chaney already knew Greg well and had connected with him at a very personal level. In only a minute or two, Coach could convey that he understood Greg's fears and apprehensions — and ennobled him to rise above them and embrace the challenge of an unfamiliar cold university, being away from his family, the temptation to hang out with kids who seemed like a lot of fun but would make it harder not easier to do what he had come to Temple to do — fulfill his dreams.

Alex was another unexpected visitor. Coach used us as a platform to celebrate one of his "favorite sons." "Now here is the real thing, the best of the best, someone who really makes me proud," Coach nearly shouted with unbridled enthusiasm. "Alex here has never missed a class, never been in trouble. He helps the young players, tells the truth, a real model. I'm so proud of him."

With that speech, Coach grabbed Alex by the shoulder, twisted him around, and gave him a short hit on the arm and a kiss on the back of the neck as only a loving father could do. After Alex left the room, Chaney threw his hands up in wonder. He shared a personal story about Alex and his family, an anecdote that illustrated beyond any doubt that his concern for each player — and for each player's potential — extended well beyond the limits of the basketball court.

Coach knew the very best of who each player was and the very best of what each player aspired to be. In Coach's eyes, each young man could see his full potential reflected and affirmed. It was out there, even before the player had the courage to be the dream, rather than merely pushed off to the side as a footnote in wistful, private, when-I-have-nothing-more-important-to-consider conversations. In less than a minute, with an audience present, Coach communicated his affirmation to Alex in a way that Alex would find complimentary and caring.

Rigor. Although it's been nearly a decade since Coach Chaney retired, sports writers still talk about his Hall of Fame accomplishments, even though his team never actually won a national championship, despite an impressive win-loss record. They all cite the same facts when they talk about the Chaney success story. The 5:30 AM practices, the no-exceptions code of conduct, the high academic standards, his insistence on integrity that was so inviolate that he actually put himself on suspension when it looked like his actions might have crossed a line. They talk about the discipline that was the hallmark of a Chaney team — discipline that would be impressive for any college team, but especially so for a group of young athletes who come from disadvantaged tough neighborhoods and broken homes, for whom college basketball isn't a ticket to the NBA but to a college education and a chance at a better life and a more fulfilling dream.

Risk. The hidden side of Coach Chaney's secret sauce — the one you don't see in the news reports or the TV sound-bites — is the depth of his caring for his players. His rock-sold belief in their potential, not just for success on the court but for success in life. His investment of time, care, attention, even before they prove to him that they are worthy of that time, care, attention and have "delivered the goods" in big plays on the court, having each other's back with teammates or making grades in the classroom. Coach has so much trust, faith, belief in his players that he's focused on potential more than risk — and on positive imaging that sees them successful in later life rather than flirting with bankruptcy as a college basketball has-been. He's all-in, investing in their success. And trusts older players, like Alex, to step up and take on extra responsibility with younger players.

Candor. Because Chaney's been there — a poor person of color who didn't have the same opportunities that middle-class college kids have — he knows the risks. The temptations. The downsides of using physical power, size, athletic prowess, charm to get a "pass" on achievements that don't come as easily and feed into their fears and insecurities. He talks straight, with his players and with the media, about the hand that fate has dealt his players. About the opportunity they have. And about the pitfalls they'll face — in themselves, in society, even in the University — to make the most of the opportunity. Ask Coach for an opinion and you'll get it. And, if you don't ask, you'll get it the same way, straight up and undiluted. Coach isn't concerned with the political consequences of speaking the truth. He isn't concerned with whether you'll like him or will like what he has to say. Instead, he asks, "Is this truth that needs to be heard — to serve a higher Purpose, rekindle Will, strengthen Rigor, ennoble and uplift people to take the Risks that will ignite brilliance and actualize their full potential?"

Will. Energy, enthusiasm, passion, hope. And constant reminders to "be the dream," withstand the pressure, project "winning as an attitude." These are the antidotes to fear, pessimism, and the nagging self-doubt that many gifted players have — when they are asked to stretch beyond their athletic and physical abilities, which are outstanding, and develop their mental and emotional abilities. It's clear to Chaney that what got his players here, *to* Temple, won't yet be enough to get them *through* Temple and beyond, to the dream of a better life. It's clear that each of them has great potential to break free of the trendline that can leave them as a college basketball has-been and can squander all of the hopes and dreams, the years of sacrifice, that their families made to get them here.

Purpose. Why, as Besse observed, do so many of Coach's players continue to seek his counsel, 5, 10, 20 years after they left his team? Because he keeps them grounded. Reminds them what "success" really means. In nearly every interview Chaney gave, he talked about wins and losses not in terms of games or championships — and he talked about the strength of the Temple program not in terms of celebrity endorsements or endowments — but in terms of inflection points created. Lives set on a different trajectory. Talented young men who lifted themselves above poverty and racism, to create a better future for themselves and their families. And give back some of what he gave to their own communities.

The US Marine Captain — in an office without walls

The Captain was responsible for Leadership Development in a billion-dollar corporation and invited us to present Power Up Brilliance workshops as part of their core leadership curriculum. We spent seven days with him over a three month period, all before his unit was activated for deployment to Iraq for Gulf War II. What we learned from watching the Captain in those months leading up to deployment taught us as much about powering up brilliance as we ever gave his groups.

"Hey there, warrior," he answered the cellphone, with the same "glad-to-hear-from-you" spirit that Coach Chaney showed when Besse appeared at the door with a visitor. No matter what was going on in the planning meeting or workshop, it was clear to everyone that the call was a welcome interruption and that the rest of us should pick up the slack, keep things moving and let him give the caller the attention that he deserved.

On the occasions when we weren't keeping a workshop moving, the Captain would put his hand over the phone, talking loudly enough for the caller to still hear him. "This is Marvin," he would tell us, with a 20-30 second description of Marvin's greatest talents and the reasons he was glad to have Marvin in his command.

"Warrior," we heard the Captain say, "I don't know what to tell you. I read the same news reports you do, and I'd imagine I'll find out about our orders and deployment about the same time you will. What can you do to prepare? Tell your wife and kids how much you love them. Be as kind as you can. Look at everything that needs fixing around your house and get it all done. Be affectionate, forgiving and patient."

It was the only time — before then or since then — that I've ever seen love like that channeled through a cellphone. The Captain knew each Marine's family, their personal situation, their fears and, most important, their hopes and dreams. His Purpose wasn't just going into battle with them, achieving the military mission or bringing them back alive. It was being a force in helping them live their dreams.

"Everyone thinks that courage is about facing death without flinching. But almost anyone can do that. Almost anyone can hold their breath and not scream for as long as it takes to die.

"Courage is about facing life without flinching. I don't mean the times when the right path is hard, but glorious at the end. I'm talking about enduring the boredom, the messiness and the inconvenience of doing what is right."

- Robin Hobb, The Right Ship

Chapter 10
Luminous Efficiency,
Peripheral Vision and Relational Connectivity

Conventional wisdom on change management tells luminaries to slow down so laggards can catch their breath and advises them to let Luddites voice their worst fears, so they can see there is "nothing to fear but fear itself." But there's one problem with this advice. It's out of touch with external realities. Regulators and payers won't wait for medical device or drug companies to "get comfortable" with new standards. They simply won't put the product on formulary. Investors won't wait — before deciding to bet their capital on a more promising venture.

Growing more concerned and impatient with this advice, yesterday Rafi fired his coach and told his innovation leadership forum that he would no longer attend its weekly conference calls. "Their advice doesn't work for me," he said. "They don't get it. In our business, we run fast and lean. Instead of telling me to slow down, reach out to Luddites and disbelievers, hand-hold and cajole," he groused, "they should be talking about lighting a fire under laggards and getting them to step up and pick up the pace."

"We simply don't have time for meticulous planning," Rafi said, or for deliberations about 'how someone will feel when his or her precious ideas are challenged or rejected,' and for hours devoted to private kid-glove ennobling uplifting conversations. Anyone who's ever worked with me knows how deeply I care about the members of my team," he added, seeing the look on his ex-coach's face. "But this is a time when we need to speed things up, and devote payroll and bandwidth to progress, rather than hand-holding. Peripheral vision is fine, but we need to look straight ahead and push hard to get to the next milestone and bring cash into this enterprise."

Rafi isn't the first business leader who's impatient with conventional wisdom about change. There isn't always time for long uplifting dialogues. Sometimes we need brilliance to "just happen," automatically, without anyone sticking their head above the parapets, wrestling down tough issues, defying entropy or inertia. Sometimes, we don't have time for the extra email, telephone contact or international flight to bring together the right players. Or for conversation after conversation ennobling a fearful and reluctant Luddite to unleash his or her potential and Power Up Brilliance.

Enter a hardware store to buy light bulbs and you'll find them rated by luminous efficiency. Bulbs with high ratings generate more lumens of brilliance with little energy, and give off little residual heat. In our cross-functional teams and matrix networks, we have to manage power and bandwidth wisely. We also need a high level of luminous efficiency. Without having to ask. Here's how to engineer that kind of connectivity.

A systemwide perspective: Looking past narrow holes in the wall

Years ago, we did a consulting project to improve productivity and product quality in a potato chip factory that was famous for selling its product in brown and tan 20-litre (5 gallon) cans. The company had two factories using the same technology and the same production process.

When we toured one of the two plants, people lit up and smiled when they saw us, rather than averting their eyes and turning away. They were eager to show us how things worked. Operators paid attention and materials handlers walked with a bounce in their step. In focus groups, they talked with pride about their jobs. Unfortunately, that plant had the far lower productivity and quality statistics than its sister operation to the South.

When we brought the department heads in the low-productivity, high-pride plant together, they each talked about their respective operations and the resources needed to keep things running smoothly. The head of the Can Wash department pleaded that he needed two materials handlers to take cans off the assembly line and stack them up, when the conveyor belt slowed down. The head of the Filling department needed two materials handlers to retrieve cans and put them on the conveyor. The two departments were adjacent to each other, separated by a 70 cm thick stone wall, but they might as well have been on different continents.

When we mapped the flow of cans through the entire system, the department heads were surprised how easy it was to boost productivity. They didn't need a consultant or engineering expert to see the solution. Shut off one can-wash machine and tinker with the speed of the conveyor in the filling department. Presto. Four materials handlers could be reassigned to jobs where they could add value, rather than running after a too-empty or overflowing-beyond-capacity conveyor, like an old episode from the TV Classic, *I Love Lucy.*

In his book, *The goal,* Eliyahu Goldratt (2012) talked about goals that seem impossible, simply because we look within walls rather than viewing work flows from a systemwide perspective and asking, "What constraints are problems to solve (e.g., varying the speed and output of the can-wash machines) — and what constraints are the 'givens' that we have to live with and work around (e.g., the speed and output of the can-filling machines)?"

Lowering activation barriers

Marvin Weisbord and Sandra Janoff (2010) made a dramatic discovery, building on large-group organization problem-solving and strategic planning designs that were pioneered by Professor Rod Napier. If you bring together stakeholders from the entire value chain — customers, suppliers, regulators, workers and others — you can construct a far more robust, executable and profitable strategic plan than relying on a small inner circle of senior managers to build the scenarios. A Future Search Conference, as Weisbord renamed Napier's method, might include dozens, or hundreds, of stakeholders. It is a bit chaotic, but incredibly powerful — because it lowers activation barriers, and gets people who do not normally interact to sharpen up each other's thinking and learn from each other's diverse perspectives.

If you are the orchestrator of a cross-functional team, you may not convene an off-site conference. But that does not prevent you from bringing diverse advisors and executors together and lifting their periscopes, so they see their efforts from a broader systemwide horizon. If you are orchestrating, it's important for you to let teammates know what cues to watch for — and when they need to come in, on time and in sync for smooth co-ordination.

When Oren Becker and his partners designed the drug discovery engine at Predix, they turned conventional thinking on its ear by looking across the system. If you could get computational chemistry, biology, medicinal chemistry and other disciplines to work in parallel and co-ordination rather than in sequence and independently, they reasoned, you should be able to accelerate progress by sharpening up each other's thinking as you go, rather than making iterative adjustments. And by killing compounds that are not likely to yield approvable, reimbursable products — based on computer models, which are far less expensive than laboratory or animal studies.

Becker left Predix and is now CEO of Dynamix Pharmaceuticals, named to reflect the dynamic tension that exists when a molecular team operates with brilliance. The key to success, Oren contends, is lowering the activation barriers — in physical proximity, in information sharing and also the way people interact — so teammates function as a seamless network, and push each other to find better and more elegant solutions, rather than presenting to executives and waiting for the CEO or CTO to be the only ones with the authority or line of sight to look across the system and ask the tough questions.

Orchestrators are the linkers who bring the right luminaries together, so you have the right luminaries to address the right issues. And they equip teammates to push, challenge, critique and probe for the best solutions, not necessarily the easy, obvious or politically expedient solutions — with ennobling straight talk, using the formula you saw in Chapters 6 and 7, to lift each other's courage.

But a key test of courage for orchestrators is the one that Becker discovered and mastered, as CTO of Predix and Dynamix. Let go. You don't have to be the luminary. You can rely on the intelligence and insight of the luminaries around you. Like our own consulting team in the potato chip factory, Becker knew that the CTO didn't have to be the one to ask all of the tough questions or provide all of the breakthrough answers — as long as you brought the right braintrust together, gave them access to the right data and created the right level of dynamic tension.

Relational co-ordination

Conventional wisdom tells us that teams operate most efficiently when everyone knows what job they are expected to do, where their authority begins and ends, and what rules they have to follow. According to Brandeis University professor Jody Hoffer Gittell, that is a nice beginning but it is not enough. Dr Gittell (2009) systematically studied the interaction of airline flight crews and their impact on on-time performance, cost-efficiency, handling difficult and unexpected situations and job stress.

Flight crews with truly stellar performance, she found, had a strong sense of connectivity. Rather than sticking to union contracts that prescribe strict work rules and role definitions, and erect mental or contractual stone walls between job functions, they look across the system. They see who depends on them for what and flex their roles, their workload, their authority — to give colleagues what they need, when they need it. The result is a system that adapts to circumstances — weather, ground equipment, passengers, Murphy's Law, stuff — to make the planes run on time.

In her next studies, Gittell asked how relational co-ordination affected the performance of another group of workers who do time-sensitive and zero-margin-for-error work in close quarters — namely, Operating Room staffs. Here, too, she found that role clarity and a clear sense of "who is responsible for what" is not enough to distinguish a decent track record from a stellar one. Instead, stellar success was achieved by the OR crews who knew how to look *beyond* their own roles and, mentally, could take down the walls between functions. They achieved fewer delays and shorter waits, fewer mistakes and higher patient satisfaction ratings. And higher levels of employee engagement, since teammates felt welcomed rather than resented when they crossed boundaries between roles and went the extra meter to fill the gaps, when they saw something going wrong.

Orchestrators may bring teammates together for relational connectivity and may alleviate the activation barriers, so they know that it's their job to look across the system. But they can't direct it or command it. They can't oversee every interaction or pull the strings to say who talks to whom, coordinates on what, shares equipment or shoulders their share of the load. When you look at a team with a high level of relational connectivity, in the ER or the airplane, the drug development lab or one of our online team problem-solving simulations, it looks like magic. It just happens. But, with every exchange, backward glance, suggestion and criticism, sigh and shrug, the connectivity is shaped — from the bottom-up and from the middle out, as every individual makes his or her presence felt in the network.

I've got your back — not a stab in the back

Todd Wallach, CEO of Jerusalem- and Philadelphia-based Molecular Detection, talked about the dissatisfaction he encountered, when he made his first visit to the Israeli site where the company was founded. "I was tempted to fire every one of them," Wallach said, with a big grin, "until I looked past the bravado and arrogance and listened to what they were actually saying. They asked smart probing questions. Weren't intimidated by my authority. Knew the business and the technology. And demanded decisions that would ensure success rather than telling the board what they wanted to hear." Wallach came home wow'd by their level of initiative, their insight and their keen awareness of how one part of the company — in Philadelphia — impacted the other, in Jerusalem, and vice-versa.

We've coached hundreds of foreign executives about assignments that put them in charge of Israeli design, discovery and business development teams. Successful leaders, like Wallach, are turned on rather than threatened by the level of relational connectivity they see in Israeli teams that look beyond the walls that separate one location from another, one department from another, one level of the organization from another. Executives like Wallach — like OR physicians and charge nurses in rooms with high levels of relational connectivity — don't need to clamp down or rein them in, but stand ready to channel their energies so they don't go off the rails or go rogue. They trust that their teammates "have their backs" when they speak up and say, "Here's an idea" or "Here's a solution to a problem you don't yet see" — and don't suspect them of upstaging them or undermining their authority.

The result is exactly what Rafi wanted to see — quick action, rather than endless deliberation or hand-holding — even when someone crossed the boundary in a way that was sharp or tense, or that countermanded someone else's authority. Brilliance, with a high level of luminous efficiency and very little residual heat.

To create this kind of give and take with focus and systemwide perspective, orchestrators — and the teams who come together on their watch — work together with:

- **Purpose.** On Southwest Airlines' (and El Al's) planes, crews put on-time performance ahead of narrow work rules. In the ORs of highly productive hospitals, physicians and nurses put patient safety and timeliness ahead of a "you-mind-your-business-I-mind-mine" definition of professional respect. In companies like Molecular Detection, they put R&D timelines and commercialization ahead of organizational hierarchies. This doesn't "just happen." It's the result of people taking the effort to learn what really drives the business — or, in the case of the OR, what really saves lives — and feeling personally connected to achieving that vision. And it's the result of management sharing that information with teammates in a way that makes it easy to understand.

- **Will.** Humor, banter, smiles. High-energy music. There's a magic to happiness, to an upbeat optimistic mood, that makes it easier to take criticism— even if it's pointed. Or to yield authority or positional power and allow someone else to encroach on your turf. That's why joking around is part of Southwest's success formula and why the music system and ambience are an integral part of every OR. With a gesture and glance, you cut the tension and lift the mood. You can convey your confidence, even when you are asking, "Please step aside and let me handle this" or, "Would you mind covering something extra for me?"

- **Rigor.** Becker's requirements are higher than most other drug discovery operations. He expects top-notch scientists not just to know their own jobs, but the entire process as well. To know where they fit in and what's upstream and downstream of them, as well as what's on their bench and computer screen. To anticipate knock-on impacts and interdependencies. He not only expects peripheral vision, he also invests in it — so specialists have knowledge that is narrow and deep in their own fields, and broad across the entire drug discovery and drug development process.

- **Risk.** Nothing takes more trust than working interdependently in close quarters. For the Head of the Can Wash Department, relinquishing one machine and four full-time employees would have been unthinkable if she were consumed with worry about loss of status, promotion opportunity or prestige. For Todd Wallach, as CEO, dynamic tension was not just necessary, but welcome, when he "got" the fact that his Israeli employees cared deeply about the business and wanted him to be "their best CEO ever." Before you encroach on someone else's turf, make sure you convey your heartfelt commitment to making them look good and to seeing them succeed.

- **Candor.** Contrast the openness that it takes for the OR staff who scored high on relational co-ordination with the defensiveness that the Head of Chemistry, Amal, exhibited in Chapter 7. Contrast Todd Wallach's openness when his new R&D team challenged his assumptions with a hundred CEOs who don't listen to what is said and defend their authority. It's one thing to say you want Candor, probing, asking the tough questions, coming up with the best answers — to ignite brilliance. It's another thing when the very openness you wish for makes you say, "Ouch."

The world is a dangerous place, not because of those who do evil but because of those who look on and do nothing.

- Albert Einstein

Chapter 11
The King and Queen of Korea:
Ignite Brilliance, Power Innovation

Some national leaders are legends because they Powered Up Brilliance and set their nations on a different trajectory. Most of them are remembered for leading their countries to victory in war or through a bitter fight to throw off colonial rule and gain independence. King Sejong and Queen Soheon are different. When they inherited the throne in Korea, the peninsula was prosperous and at peace. Yet, as they looked at the state of their Kingdom, they were painfully aware that Korea had much more potential. They were like the CEOs who participated in the IBM study, which we cited at the beginning of this book. How, Sejong and Soheon asked, could they Power Up Brilliance — and transform Korea from a sleepy quaint agrarian outpost, living in the shadows of China and Japan, to a self-sufficient source of breakthrough technology and innovation.

Sejong was a scholar, an empiricist — in today's vernacular, a "nerd." He was an unlikely choice for King, having no physical or military prowess. He spoke softly. Listened intently. And while his wife, Queen Soheon, honored Sejong's position as titular head of the family in public, in private Sejong respected her as in intellectual equal. In their own quiet, understated, intellectual way, Sejong and Soheon set the Kingdom on a radically different trajectory, decreed an inflection point and said, "March or die." Six hundred years after they assumed the throne, their reign is still considered the birth of Modern Korea.

At the age of 22, King Sejong and Queen Soheon the Great inherited the throne. The obstacle to brilliance, they determined after careful study, was the country's pitifully low literacy rate — far lower than any other Asian country. It would not be an easy problem to solve. There was no alphabet to write in Korean and the pictographic 400+ character system adopted in China and Japan was far too complex for pragmatic, impatient Koreans to learn quickly.

Within two decades, under their leadership, Korea was transformed. The change the set in motion has endured, 600 years later. South Korea still has one of the highest literacy rates in the world. There is no doubt that it has been — and still is — a technology, innovation and manufacturing powerhouse. It was here that movable type, mass-produced reading material, universal education, democratic rule were invented — years before Gutenberg. To power literacy, Korea produced rapid advances in nearly every craft, from metallurgy to chemical formulations for ink, paper, agriculture and medicines. All sparked by a shy, unassuming, softspoken King and Queen.

How did they Power Up Brilliance?

At a time when the power of the monarch was absolute and subjects could be held in submission by ignorance, poverty and fear, King Sejong and Queen Soheon the Great were driven by a vision of education, prosperity and empowerment for the ordinary citizens of their country. And by solving problems, rather than pretending that they didn't exist or that they didn't really matter.

They commissioned several innovators to devise written alphabets for the Korean language and tested those prototypes with children. When they were satisfied that one system was easy enough for even the simplest of their subjects to learn, they rolled it out across the kingdom. Sejong and Soheon expected their subjects to embrace the new symbols. But, as we know, change doesn't happen just because the person at the top has a vision and knows what's needs to be done. Even as the monarchs of a feudal society, King Sejong and Queen Soheon had a tough time getting their subjects to learn to read and write using the symbols they had invented and pilot tested.

According to The Legend of King Sejong and Queen Soheon...

> *"Important people in all the cities and villages looked at the symbols and whispered among themselves. 'We cannot use them,' they told one another. 'King Sejong and Queen Soheon are great, but the gods are even greater. Koreans have always used the Chinese way of writing, because the gods will it.'*

> *"Many weeks later, [Royal Minister] Chong-In-ji told the king the sad news. 'People don't like the new alphabet. They say the gods have blessed only the Chinese way of writing.'*

> *"The gods can bless more than one way of writing!' Sejong and Soheon declared. 'We must think of how to show people this truth.'*

But no matter how hard they and the scholars of their court tried, they could not think of a way to do this.

Thus was born a monumental change management dilemma. And a mobilization of complex, networked matrix structures to solve never-before-attempted technology hurdles. On a par with the American race for space in the 1960s, the rebuilding of Zion in the 20th Century, the Chinese economic revolution of the early 2000s.

Even in modern society, it is not easy to teach adults to read. Becoming literate is a frustrating task, even if you already have mastered one alphabet and now have to learn to navigate in a new one. In modern society, those who don't know how to read and write recognize that they are operating at a real disadvantage. But, in Sejong's and Soheon's day, there was safety in numbers. Those who couldn't read and write in the new Hangul alphabet could take refuge in the fact that almost all of their fellow countrypeople also couldn't read and write.

As the official monarchs of the Korean nation, King Sejong and Queen Soheon knew they had the power to demand compliance and force their subjects to learn the new language. But they were wise enough to know that forced compliance wouldn't be enough to get the populace to use the written language and make it part of their daily lives. They understood that the courage to transform Korean society couldn't be ordered or decreed, not even by the all-powerful King and Queen.

If the Korean people didn't have the courage to confront their illiteracy and Power Up Brilliance, Sejong and Soheon knew it wouldn't succeed – let alone take root in the society and outlast their lifetime. If the people didn't invert hegemony and transform their view of Korean culture vis-à-vis the more powerful and revered Chinese language, the new symbols would be dismissed as the ravings of a self-impressed monarch rather than embraced as a gift to the people. What's more, King Sejong and Queen Soheon knew that, as King and Queen, very few of their subjects would have the courage to tell them the truth, like Chong-In-ji had done, and would create the illusion that the new alphabet was taking root, lest the King and Queen be displeased and dishonored.

With benefit of hindsight, we see that King Sejong's and Queen Soheon's experiment was indeed a success. The Hangul alphabet is still used as the written Korean language. Korea's literacy rate is among the highest in the world. And, far from sowing the seeds of the overthrow and destruction of the Choson dynasty, King Sejong and Queen Soheon left behind the foundation for a ruling dynasty that endured for over 500 years.

But success looks different in retrospect, when we already know how the drama plays out, than it does when you do not know what lies over the next hilltop. Looking forward from 1443, when King Sejong and Queen Soheon introduced the Hangul alphabet or from 1446, when the script was promulgated, the experiment looked much tenuous. From what has been pieced together in historical documents and Korean folklore, it looks as if King Sejong and Queen Soheon the Great had all 5 Activators firmly in their mind and in their heart – and imbued them in others:

- **Purpose: Powered Up to pursue a lofty and audacious goal.** "The sounds of our country's language are different from those of the Middle Kingdom [China] and are not confluent with the sounds of characters. Therefore, among the ignorant people, there have been many who, having something they want to put into words, have in the end been unable to express their feelings. I have been distressed because of this, and have newly designed 28 letters, which I wish to have everyone practice at their ease and make convenient for their daily use." Everyone. Daily use. Lofty and audacious? A new inflection point that broke free of the old trendline? You bet.

- **Will: Powered Up to inspire hope, spirit and promise.** According to the legend of King Sejong and Queen Soheon, there were times in the mobilization of the kingdom where they were discouraged and lost heart. They expected the new alphabet to be embraced enthusiastically as their gift to a grateful nation. They tested it to make sure it could be easily learned. Still, it was not embraced and few had the will to overcome their illiteracy. Legend has it that, until the symbols were seen etched in the bark of the trees of the forest and those etchings were taken as the will of the gods, neither the "ignorant people" nor the noblemen in Sejong's and Soheon's court were willing to endure the frustration of learning and teaching the new language. Despite their frustration, Sejong and Soheon had to act "as if" the experiment would succeed, show their confidence in ordinary Koreans to do the heavy lifting to create that success, and build energy and momentum.

- **Rigor: Powered Up to get the right people working on the right improvements with the right connectivity.** Institutionalizing the Hangul alphabet took more than a royal decree. To establish letters that would be more than a handwritten curiosity out of the reach of the common people, King Sejong and Queen Soheon also had to invent a way of transforming the language from calligraphy to reproducible type. Printing with woodblocks was impractical, because only 20to 30 copies could be made from a single woodcut. Unless typography could be improved to meet the demand for a greater number and variety of printed texts, Sejong and Soheon reasoned, the language would not endure. Thus, they assembled a brain-trust of the best and brightest technicians and formed task forces and enterprise teams charged with the task of improving the typeface and moving from wood to metallurgy. The advances in metallurgy brought 15th Century Korea to a level of industrial development – in tools, farm implements and printing – that Europe wouldn't achieve for another century or more.

- **Risk: Powered Up to trust, empower and invest in relationships.**
  Many of the senior ministers in King Sejong's and Queen Soheon's court warned about the dangers of universal literacy. If the masses are able to express their true feelings and thoughts freely, the ministers warned, how can we maintain our power and control? It was a radical, unprecedented experiment and a giant leap of faith. Who knew what people would do with their newfound power and independence, once the written language took on a life of its own? To mitigate the risks and truly empower the people, Sejong and Soheon instituted a series of land reforms and tax reforms that were commensurate with the freedoms that a literate and educated people should enjoy. They introduced the first system of healthcare reform as well. Rather than shrinking from the risk or underestimating the risk of literacy, they embraced it – and prepared society to function effectively with newfound power and independence. They strengthened the authority and legitimacy of the Choson dynasty by building the Korean national consciousness and raising it to a level of freedom and democratic

achievement that would be unprecedented for many centuries in Asian or Western history.

- **Candor: Powered Up to speak and hear the truth.** King Sejong and Queen Soheon knew that the common people – the very subjects they most wanted to reach – would not dare to tell them the truth, if it were something they did not want to hear. So Sejong disguised himself as a commoner and went among the people, to hear firsthand how the new alphabet was received and to become more aware of the difficulties and skepticism that had to be overcome. Armed with honest, firsthand feedback, King Sejong and Queen Soheon convened meetings of their inner cabinet to deal with the problems and find solutions. Today, over 500 years later, Sejong and Soheon are still revered — for the courage to listen openly, and use what they learned for generative adaptive solution-seeking probing and dialogue.

In modern times, we also are impressed with leaders who strengthen their position of power and influence by enabling and empowering their followers, rather than subjugating them. And with leaders who refuse to take, "No, it can't be done" for an answer, and press for generative adaptive solutions.

We admire the Purpose, Will, Rigor, Risk and Candor of leaders like Yitzchak Rabin (z"l), Anwar Sadaat (z"l), Shimon Peres, King Abdullah and Queen Rania of Jordan in contrast to those who speak of peace but continue to exploit their people and promulgate fear rather than opportunity and liberty. We admire the integrity of military heroes like

General Romeo Dallaire, who pushed himself to do more than present an illusion or appearance of peacekeeping as commander of Canadian and UN Forces in Rwanda, and US Gen Norman Schwartzkofpf (z"l) who, even before he was a General in Vietnam, had a zero-tolerance stance toward the racism that he saw in some military circles and the courage to stand by those convictions. We admire the courage of heroes like Ernest Shackelton (z"l), who refused to abandon his shipwrecked crew in the wasteland of Antarctica and did whatever he could to imbue his ill-fated team with the Purpose, Will, Rigor, Risk and Candor to survive the hardships, even when it would have been easier to admit defeat and return to the warmth and comfort of England. We may not be called to stand on a stage as large as theirs, but hopefully we can be inspired by them — and can ignite brilliance by lifting people higher rather than leaving them alone, to settle for what's routine and comfortable.

In 20/20 hindsight, we know that the officers of Enron and Worldcom were wrong when they refused to admit that their companies were losing money rather than posting a healthy profit. And that the management of BP and NASA might have averted catastrophes if they had imbued the courage that engineers needed to say, "Houston, we have a problem," rather than just following orders. We see Apple riding high on product innovation and read reports of questionable labor and sales practices in the US and China — and wonder whether they will turn the corner quickly enough to avert a bigger problem later.

We also know that the corporate officers of Johnson & Johnson were right, when they had the courage to pull the entire supply of Tylenol off the shelves and take the hit on their bottom line. We know that Quaker

Chemical was right when it invested heavily in customer partnerships and in the people who are smart, hardworking and ethical enough to "walk the talk" of demanding company values. As was ARAMARK, empowering managers to build on client relationships and build multi-service, multi-site service agreements. Along with hundreds of companies that reinvented themselves and created whole new industries, like a Phoenix rising from the ashes of the economic meltdown of 2008-2010.

But, again, this is courage viewed in hindsight. The officers of Johnson and Johnson, ARAMARK, Quaker Chemical and countless others refused to compromise their sense of Purpose, Will, Rigor, Risk and Candor in the face of an inflection point that any of us hope we will never encounter. When Merck recalled Vioxx, because it was the right thing to do, they didn't know how it would turn out, any more than General Schwartzkopf knew whether refusing to enter an officer's club that denied entry to South Vietnamese Army officers would red-line his military career. Cautious advisors warned King Sejong and Queen Soheon that all this brilliance and power could result in a palace revolt, which they would be powerless to put down. Yet, Sejong and Soheon stayed the course, believing in the best intentions of the Korean people but not knowing, for sure, how their subjects would handle the freedom and responsibility that came with literacy and reform

Few of us face the awesome responsibilities of a head of state, a monarch, a general or the CEO of a major corporation. In a past era, these were the figures who needed courage. The rest of us were the benefactors who followed the course they charted – or were victims of their lack of courage.

But newfound freedoms, knowledge and opportunities only improve the human condition if we Power Up higher levels of Brilliance. Those who grew up in post-literate Korea needed a higher level of brilliance to deal with more complex realities than those who grew up as "an ignorant people." It wasn't just King Sejong and Queen Soheon who needed a higher level of Purpose, Will, Rigor, Risk and Candor. It was the common 15th Century Korean as well who needed a higher level of…

- **Purpose**: To pursue the lofty and audacious goal of becoming literate and helping others to do the same, one family and one village at a time
- **Will**: To inspire hope, spirit and promise in the face of frustration, to persevere until they had learned the Hangul alphabet and could use it fluently
- **Rigor**: To mobilize the right people to work the right issues and make advances, by creating new reading materials, new technologies and new networks
- **Risk**: To trust, empower and invest in relationships and embrace newfound freedom with a sense of civic pride and responsibility
- **Candor**: To speak and hear the truth in order to get help with the new alphabet, to provide feedback, and challenge the status-quo

What can we learn from Sejong and Soheon and their people?

Not everyone is lucky enough to work in the shadow of an executive team or CEO as visionary, enlightened and benevolent as King Sejong and Queen Soheon. Still, it's hard to imagine any modern organization in which workers don't have new freedom, knowledge, mobility, opportunities. By necessity, matrix and team structures are replacing or at least supplementing chains-of-command and hierarchies. Those at the top often don't know as much as those "in the trenches." And we all have discretion – to stretch, reach out and capitalize on opportunities for our enterprises or let opportunities get away.

Followers rely on leaders for vision and inspiration, access and sponsorship. That's as true today as it was in Sejong's and Soheon's time. Now as then, we suffer the consequences when our leaders aren't enlightened and when they stifle rather than ignite brilliance, as the employee-shareholders of BP and Enron will attest. And we profit when they see the future and go all-in to take the enterprise into the next era, like Dr C.

Leaders are also more dependent on their followers. A new alphabet is useless if people don't learn it and use it. State-of-the-art connectivity and online idea-exchanges are worthless if they are not embraced and if posts are not shared. Changes happen quickly and require too much knowledge and problem-solving skill for everything to be detailed in a standard operating procedures manual or controlled from headquarters. Stock options have no value unless people subscribe and see value for the future.

In 15th Century Korea, the partnerships that had to be forged between Sejong and Soheon and their people were truly extraordinary. Without such partnerships and the networks and ensembles that were mobilized to connect, share and challenge each other and build on one another's discoveries, none of Sejong's and Soheon's epic accomplishments would have been possible.

For 21st Century fast-growing African countries like Kenya to throw off the yoke of colonialism and build a new and uniquely African generation of entrepreneurship and environmentally sustainable development, a new social contract needs to be forged between those with power and those who aspire to use power wisely. The experiment is still underway, just as it was in the late years of Sejong's and Soheon's reign in Korea. The experiment is far from a tipping point that is self-sustaining. For those who stay and contribute to taking the country of Kenya forward — and for those in the Kenyan diaspora who come home to add their talents, capital, energy and ethics to the inflection points that are under construction, it takes enormous courage.

In 21st Century corporations, CEOs see that brilliance is the most essential human quality that is needed to break free of old trendlines and create new inflection points that lift the enterprise to new levels of success. To ignite that brilliance, we need the same kind of partnerships that Sejong and Soheon fostered — and the same level of courage. We need to find ways to make the extraordinary ordinary.

In corporate failures and setbacks, such as the ones we have witnessed at BP, Renault, Enron, Arthur Anderson, among others, there was too little courage too late. Even in public organizations like the FBI and NASA, we have seen what happens when people who have mission-critical information are too fearful to speak up. We've seen how brilliance is stifled when the seduction of leaders is more important than fulfilling the organization's Purpose.

In each of these cases, the "monarchs" claimed that they didn't know what was going on in their royal courts. King Sejong and Queen Soheon, in contrast, didn't wait for the truth to come to them. Only after they gathered intelligence by mingling among their people did they reveal their identities in public displays that said, "Thank you for honoring us by bringing forward the obstacles, the difficulties and the breakthrough solutions that will equip us to live up to our incredible potential as Koreans. Thank you for telling us the truth."

Even in the presence of a King Sejong and Queen Soheon, it takes courage to embrace new freedoms and opportunities, thrive in boundaryless flat structures. As Erich Fromm pointed out a generation ago in his epic *Escape from Freedom,* it is easier to hide in the chain of command and look to those in authority for answers than it is to find them or formulate them for yourself. It feels easier and safer to stay silent when we encounter things in our organizations that are not congruent with the stated vision or professed Core Values. We don't know, for sure, what we will face when we ask about questionable or misleading accounting or business practices, unseized opportunities and value that isn't yet leveraged effectively. If you are disengaged and treated as if you are incapable of brilliance, you may bristle at the lack of opportunity. But it takes courage to throw off the shackles and say, "I want my time in the sun."

Chapter 12
Mobilization in the Matrix:
Training to Power Up Brilliance

Leadership and team development is an industry that generates over $2 billion per year in fees, from enterprises that need to PowerUp Brilliance, accelerate innovation and drive strategy execution. In a 30+ year career in this industry, we've personally seen thousands of leaders learn to step in, reach out and speak up in hundreds of enterprises around the globe — and we've heard about hundreds more who've paid dearly for coaching and training, workshops and assessments, only to see more talk than walk. We've seen what ennobles and uplifts leaders to Power Up Brilliance. And we've seen what appeases, entertains, strokes egos — even excites and intrigues — but fails to have a lasting impact on courage and the brilliance that CEOs like yours know is needed.

In a recent conference for HR Executives sponsored by Bio, the international industry association for innovative life sciences enterprises, we convened a panel of CEOs like Dr C and asked, "How did you teach key leaders in your enterprise to Power Up Brilliance?" Their answers?

- We let them know that brilliance was **what we expected** — when they were hired, promoted and whenever we saw them lowering aspirations like fearful retreaters

- We did our best to **model the 5 Activators** — to "walk the talk" personally and got feedback from a coach, an internal HR advisor or other member of the team when we, personally, were "wimping out" or indulging fear and complacency

- We gave key leaders **tough stretch assignments** — expanded roles, new foreign markets, tough scientific or regulatory hurdles, demanding partnerships, all with enterprise-critical consequences, and relied on them to learn by doing.

- We provided **support and mentoring** — with outside coaches and workshops and with internal supervisors and mentors who could show them the way.

The Cenrer for Creative Leadership (CCL) asked a similar question. They surveyed hundreds of corporate executives and asked, "How did you learn to lead?" The overwhelming majority talked about lessons learned from a formative experience, a formidable business challenge, from challenges they faced in an out-of-your-comfort-zone foreign assignment or cross-functional team. They described inflection points that changed their view of self, of team, of enterprise. How they got it wrong *before* they got ennobling feedback. And the humility that it took to say, "Oops!" change direction and get it right.

Dov Frohman, the retired Managing Director of Intel Israel profiled in Chapter 7, who is credited with staring down the threat of Saddam Hussein's missiles on the emerging Israel high-tech industry in Gulf War I, has said that leadership can be learned but not taught. We agree. We can give you the 5 Activators and we can tell you how others — just like you — used them as a roadmap to Power Up Brilliance. We can rehearse, practice, prepare for the personal triggers you will face — when it is tempting to be a fearful retreater rather than a non-retreater and engager. But we cannot *teach* you how to flip the switch and bring your magic to life, at moments of truth when you need it the most to create your own luck. Frohman is right. We each have to learn to do that for ourselves.

Action learning

Neuropsychology tells us we'll remember to use the 5 Activators, if we encode them into the deepest fabric of our thinking so they become almost automatic. That's what formative experiences do for us. They change the way we see things. They reshape our reflexes and our instincts. They leave us transformed. Formative experiences may actually alter the wiring in our brains, giving us better access to the sgACC — the "courage center" of the brain we described in Chapter 2 — so it's easier to flip the switch and light up that area of our cerebral cortex when we find ourselves faced with adversity, ambiguity, hierarchy traps, foreign cultures and people who rub us the wrong way when they step up and offer their brilliance.

If we want to teach leaders to Power Up Brilliance — the best way to do it is to provide formative experiences and real challenges, so leaders look inflection points in the face and literally re-think the way they respond to adversity and to colleagues who "bring them down" rather than "lift them up."

But that doesn't mean that we should throw inexperienced leaders into deep turbulent waters and say, "Sink or swim," and hope that their careers

— and the enterprise that's entrusted to them — will automatically be enriched. Or that it's enough to point them in the right direction and say, "March or die."

Pilots learn to take off and land with simulators. Surgeons practice on animals and computers and assist before they preside. Athletes do strength training to develop the right muscles. They have scrimmages to sharpen their instincts and reactions. All before they are in franchise-critical or life-or-death situations.

What. When we train business leaders to build courage, we also put them through strength training and simulation exercises. The activities are gameified, fun, interactive, hands-on. Some involve resource allocation or possibility thinking; others involve co-ordination across multiple sites and out-of-sync time zones. The pace is fast. There are limited resources, narrow channels of communication, ambiguous roles and conflicting objectives. Teams may be led into a playing field blindfolded, placed in separate rooms or seated at a computer terminal taking avatars through a sequence of decisions. Or, leaders may be given a case study, based on a real-life leadership dilemma and asked, "What would you do?"

So what. Insight, Feedback. Skill-sharpening. Assessing — and reassessing — your options, including the ones that you failed to see, when you were caught in hierarchy traps, win/win paradigms, conventional mindsets, target blindness or paralyzed by fear and reluctance. That's the point of this after-action-analysis step in the learning cycle, to debrief the

The Action Learning Formula:

What, So What, Now What

Action learning, experience works

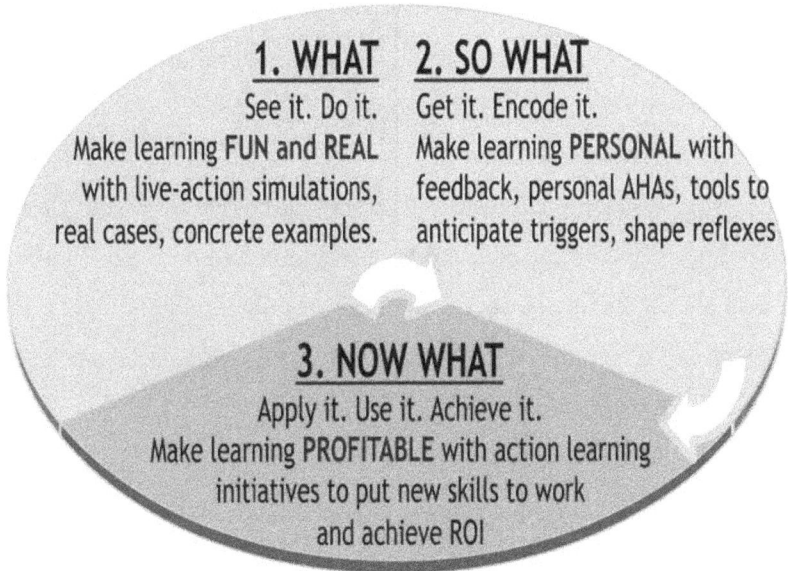

1. WHAT
See it. Do it.
Make learning FUN and REAL
with live-action simulations,
real cases, concrete examples.

2. SO WHAT
Get it. Encode it.
Make learning PERSONAL with
feedback, personal AHAs, tools to
anticipate triggers, shape reflexes

3. NOW WHAT
Apply it. Use it. Achieve it.
Make learning PROFITABLE with action learning
initiatives to put new skills to work
and achieve ROI

"We learn best from experience – by doing, reflecting, experimenting and then applying the principles.
"We achieve the best ROI when we use what we learn."

© 2013. www.courageinstitute.org • Tel: USA: +1-215-529-8918 • Israel: +972-4-3721008

opportunities that leaders seized and overlooked in the "What" phase. Deep discussions probe for this by asking leaders-in-training...

- So what did you achieve, as an individual and with your team?
- So what sparked adaptive generative can-do possibility thinking to Power Up Brilliance and accelerate innovation?
- So what inhibited or shut down brilliance, imagination and initiative?
- So what do you need to practice and perfect, drill and understand, to recondition reflexes and get control over fear centers of the brain that trigger fight-or-flight instincts?
- So what could you do better, if we hit the "reset" button and started over, faced with the same conditions, resource and time constraints?
- So how did you use resources and relationships?
- So how did you leverage the talent and Power Up Brilliance in remote dispersed parts of your network?
- So how did you overcome obstacles, fears and pressures?
- So how did you activate Purpose, Candor, Will, Rigor and Risk — in yourself and others?

Now what. This final step converts insight into action and rehearsal into on-the-job where-it-matters performance. In this last phase of learning, we enhance skill-transfer with:

- Rapid Results Projects — to achieve an enterprise-critical result in 100 days or less, mobilizing ad-hoc teams with influence and uplifting ennobling courage-building leadership rather than threats and authority
- Individual Development Plans (IDPs) — to commit to situations and skills that will bolster courage under pressure and will prepare a leader

for a more expansive, deep, complex or pressured leadership role

- Discovery Journals — to record personal insights and two or three key "aha's" about the members of the matrix team whom you need to mobilize, so you keep their sensitivities in your consciousness better than Rami, the Global Head of Sales we profiled in Chapter 4

- Team Support Contracts — to commit to specific actions that will build bridges rather than walls between your business unit and others, and will result in more optimal collaborative asset management and collaborative account management

- Strategy Execution or Change Acceleration Plans — to reach out to members of your network whom Malcolm Gladwell (2002) would call "mavens" or "connectors," so new business practices reach a tipping point and get faster adoption

- Goal Setting and Incentive Plans — to reinforce and reward courage-building practices, with a balanced scorecard that recognizes the code d'honneur that builds courage as well as bottom-line results

- Peer Coaching or Professional Mentoring — to provide live-in-action feedback and coaching from the sidelines and from the game pitch itself, rather than waiting to debrief after a key meeting, a sensitive negotiation or a "March-or-die" call to action

- Fluency on the 5 Activators — so, like a golf swing, the steps of courage-building are encoded into one fluid natural motion, that "feels right" and is authentically yours

Problem-focused vs outcome-focused leadership development

Rob was the complacent and content CEO in a family business. His VP of Sales told him that they needed a training program to Power Up Brilliance and teach up-and-coming middle managers to be innovators. But Rob was skeptical. When we interviewed Ron, he told us that he saw no need for an upgrade. He said that was already living a good life, making a respectable profit, with no cause for alarm about turbulence that might lie ahead, no matter what his niece, the VP of Sales, forewarned. Powering Up Brilliance, for Rob, was a reckless adventure, a daredevil mountain-climb, an adrenaline rush that the younger generation was overly eager to embrace, just to prove themselves worthy of their inheritance. "No, thanks," Rob said. "Count me out. We are doing quite well being an average company selling average products to average customers at average prices. We don't need to do anything more."

Try teaching innovators to Power Up Brilliance when they will encounter a top executive and principal shareholder with Rob's perspective. At best, the "What" activities will be invigorating and the "So what" debriefs will be provocative. But, by putting the brakes on the "Now what," there will be little to show for the investment in training, assessments, IDPs and coaching — no matter how enjoyable the learning process is. "Full gas neutral," we call it in Hebrew.

Leadership teams with Luddites like Ron frequently become dysfunctional. Futurists and traditionalists form opposing camps and square off against one another. One side of the Atlantic vies for hegemony against the

Corporate Headquarters on the other side. Walls become impenetrable. Disciplines and business units compete for resources. Issues get politicized. Trust is low. Fear is rampant. Training focuses on "what we have to do, to get permission or fly under the radar," not "what can do to Power Up Brilliance, get traction and boost profits with luminous efficiency."

We felt for Rob's niece and the visionary potentially brilliant leaders around her. "Can you fix Rob and the rest of our "don't-rock-the-boat" executives?" she asked, after we finished a day of interviews. We could see her pain, reflected in mournful tales about what hadn't worked, and a litany of symptoms that the victims of the dysfunction endured until they threw up their hands and resigned. She presented us with employee engagement and change-readiness scores that were woefully low — and told us how difficult it had become to recruit real stars for key positions.

"You do get it, don't you?" we asked Rob and the traditionalists on his team when we presented the results of our Power Up Brilliance Readiness Survey. We knew that we sounded a lot like Doctor Phil, the American TV counselor known for straight talk and ennobling uplifting interventions. "If you continue on this trajectory, it could have dire consequences for your family wealth and for your enterprise." Rob nodded. He acknowledged that things *had* to change — and that it was not good business to continue to operate with politics, fear, mistrust and isolated competing fiefdoms, or with a next generation of management that was on the verge of taking an exit and liquidating their shares.

After patients have their epiphany — on Doctor Phil's TV show or in real life — we'd like to believe that they get the help they need, create a new inflection point and live happily ever after. Unfortunately, even when heart surgeons talk with patients about changing a sedentary lifestyle and rich diet that could leave them dead or incapacitated, fewer than 30% follow through and change their habits. The same is true with corporations. According to research by John Kotter, fewer than half of the grand transformations that executive teams announce actually produce the breakthroughs, the brilliance and the courage that they hope to see to unleash their potential. Dysfunctions like the ones that strangled creativity and extinguished brilliance in Rob's company are hard to eradicate.

Decades before he became known as the guru of positive psychology, Professor Martin Seligman did a series of research studies about psychotherapy patients. He asked why some therapists have higher success rates than others. Seligman analyzed their treatment notes, and audiotapes of their first few treatment sessions. All therapists, he found, focus on the past and get a good diagnosis of what's wrong. They all are competent with the Diagnostic and Statistical Manual (DSM) and assign the right DSM code to their patients. They all, like Doctor Phil and like most cardiologists, give patients an emotionally cathartic epiphany — and a reason why "they have to get help — or perish."

The difference, Seligman found, was in the way therapists focused on the future. Therapists were more successful getting patients to show up for a second and third treatment session when they looked beyond what is painful, frustrating and dysfunctional, and asked about hopes, dreams, and aspirations. Seligman's data persuaded him to tell therapists to look beyond DSM and stop treating symptoms, as if analyzing pathology, asking "why," and holding it under a magnifying glass could make it go away. Get in touch with your patients' strengths, he advocated instead, and on what they want to do with those strengths — if they have the courage to change the trajectory. This was the beginning of positive psychology.

The same lessons apply to leadership consultants like us. The energy changes when we stop focusing on symptoms, frustrations and mediocrity and ask, "What would different look like?" The pace increase, eyes look up, breathing quickens. The Purpose becomes even more compelling when we drill down from vague generalities like, "communicate better" or "increase trust," and ask, "What would these improvements do for your business? Why are they not just nice-to-do, but business-critical? How will you know you are turning the corner and getting traction?" And "Why now?"

Our data and experience lead us to the same conclusion Seligman reached when he asked about therapy patients. Sponsors like Rob engage only when brilliance powers an immediate "march-or-die" business imperative — and when there's a clear, enterprise-critical ROI that the team hopes to achieve. When times get tough, it isn't enough to say, "This will make us a happier and more fulfilling place to work" unless there's also an enterprise-critical ROI that the team has to achieve by mobilizing themselves and their teams with more Purpose, Will, Rigor, Risk and Candor.

We never stop being amazed how often a disconnect occurs among HR professionals between the behavioral imperative for brilliance, high

231

performance, engagement (which most HR Directors "get") and the potential ROI. Like any other capital investment or operational expense, we need to show a robust business case to strengthen those muscles. A business owner like Rob, at best, might be intrigued by courage. But invest in it — financially and emotionally? Not unless there's a clear line of sight between brilliance and his/her bottom line.

Dr C saw the business case clearly. He got the Purpose — and could articulate it clearly. When he called his executive team together, the Activator he needed to lift first was Candor. Because his senior executives saw people coming to work and digging in, they thought the enterprise was already firing on all cylinders. They didn't see the gap — between their current trendline and the performance and innovation benchmarks needed to stay competitive.

Dr C and a small inner circle of luminaries and early adopters who "got it" put together a list of Key Performance Indicators (KPIs). Because profits were already strong, they used a Balanced Scorecard methodology — which looked at Customer Loyalty, Operational and Supply Chain Modernization and Employees' Readiness and Skill to Support Innovation. The elite inner circle of luminaries knew that profit was a lagging performance indicator. They could look ahead, like Mr B's corporation did, long before the economic meltdown — and see that the time to strengthen these foundations was now, before their backs were to the wall. Before they invested in training, hoping that leaders would "get it" and be so jazzed that they'd automatically "make things happen," Dr C's HR Director insisted on a business case.

ARAMARK's Mission One campaign, profiled in our first book, *The Courage to Act,* was a brilliant call-to-action for a next generation of high-courage leadership skills. There was a clear business case and profit motive — because it was far more profitable to sell a second, third or fourth service offering to an existing customer than to sell a brand-new service offering to a brand-new customer. If Foodservice would partner with Uniforms, and with Janitorial Services and Engineering and Security, it could break down the silos among service offerings. In theory, it made sense. In practice, it took a major mindflip for a foodservice or engineering professional to see him/herself as General Manager of aa multi-service client partnership (or, as ARAMARK called it, *unlimited* partnership) rather than a specialist in a particular line of business. Whenever a leadership team hit the wall in a training workshop and, like Rob, asked, "Why are we stretching so far beyond what's comfortable?" someone in the group would speak up and remind them what was at stake. By the second year of the program that someone was usually one of the participants, not the facilitator or sponsor of the program.

A Design Roadmap for Leadership Development

The 5 Activators are not just a roadmap for leaders who are mobilizing teams to ignite brilliance at times of adversity or uncertainty. They are also a roadmap for HR and Talent Management professionals designing Leadership Development programs. Heres's how:

233

Purpose. When you kick off your leadership program and explain to participants what we hope they'll achieve with brilliance, can you explain "why?" and "why now?" Can you tell them how success will be measured — not just in the workshop, but when you ask them to mobilize teams on the job and apply what they've learned? When you meet with the sponsors who are underwriting the investment and are freeing up time and bandwidth for workshops, team initiatives and coaching, how will you justify the ROI?

Candor. There's an adage that says, "The skills that got you here may not be all you need to get yourself to the next level." People smile and nod when they hear that. But that doesn't mean they actually feel compelled to dig in and learn, unless they really see that there's more to the future than their past success. Working with seasoned experienced leaders, we start most programs with a "disconfirmation" activity — a wake-up call that says, "Whoa! Hold on! Look how much more successful you could be, by taking your leadership skills to an even higher level!" Sometimes it's done with an exercise — where participants get caught in hierarchy traps, the bias against creativity, competitive or defensive instincts and suboptimize the team's results, which they plainly see in a forehead-slapping debrief. Sometimes it's done with their own performance trendlines, presented in a more dramatic light. For example, we did a mentoring program for top executives in a large global pharmaceutical company to take high-potential up-and-coming talent under their wings and prepare them for rapid advancement. When they came to the course, outspoken executives said, "We already do this well." But our performance data said that only one-third of their high-potentials felt that they had a mentor they could trust. We asked one question to spark an ennobling dialogue and move them above their comfortable denial: "Is it enough to be successful only 33% of the time?"

Will. Remember Seligman's research on psychotherapy — and the things we need to do, to infuse hope, optimism, spirit, enthusiasm. That's particularly important when we take a leadership team through a simulation — knowing that they'll fall into hierarchy traps, the bias against creativity, unimaginative thinking, win/lose competitiveness, target blindness, summit fever, and knowing they will fail as a result of these mental and groupthink traps. Hard-charging, high-potential, brilliant leaders don't like to fail — and like it even less when they fail publicly. The art of facilitation is giving them enough success to feed confidence and egos, and enough failure to feel compelled to take success to an even higher level. And to manage the pace, time, groupings and subgroupings to create pressure and creative tension — and not let the energy dip.

Rigor. With blended learning, leadership development can start the moment that you hit, "SEND," and invite a participant to enroll in the program. Even if you are planning only one live workshop session, you can still design a blended learning curriculum that includes...

- **Prework** — with a book, a case, a call-to-action, a webinar that entices courage-building leaders to dream bigger, lift higher, reach broader and dig deeper to power innovation and ignite brilliance
- **Action learning team mobilization initiative** — a concrete, ROI-producing business imperative that gives leaders a practical, coherent,

urgent and important opportunity to grow, expand or reposition the business with courage-building leadership skills

- **Assessments** — with a Power Up Brilliance Readiness Survey™, like the one we've included in the Appendix to this book, or a version that is available online @ www.courageadvisors.com as well as an online blog that gives participants an opportunity to share ideas, possibilities and dilemmas before coming together for their workshop

- **The workshop** (or workshops) — with skill-building and practice in mobilizing the right partners, assessing their readiness to act, ennobling them to lift higher with courage-building dialogues, and orchestrating their efforts as you hold them on belay

- **1:1 coaching and pull-through** — to equip sponsors to follow-up and pull-through action learning team mobilization initiatives in a way that builds accountability to equip orchestrators to continue sharpening their "lead-from-the-middle" skills, and to equip advisors and executors to create breakthrough innovation

Risk. The most significant thing we hear from the leaders who attend our workshops and coaching consultations is, "Wow, I tried what I practiced in our session — and it worked!" We don't take this lightly. It's a risk to follow someone else's counsel (rather than your own intuition) — especially when you are making an important presentation to investors or to your board, or are handling a sensitive or contentious issue. And if your career is on the line, like Rami, the Global Head of Sales who was responsible for the pricing initiative we described in Chapter 4, it's a risk to put your success in the hands of colleagues who seem to have other priorities. Who could blame you for being reluctant to let go, trust and empower someone else to shape key decisions that will affect your success — no matter what seemed to make sense while you were "under the spell" of a heart-to-heart trust-building discussion in a workshop? How can consultants and program sponsors increase the probability that high-courage behaviors rehearsed in workshops or coaching sessions will be transferred back to the job? With...

- **An upfront commitment.** A Head of Regulatory Affairs told his leadership team, "Here's how we'll use the Power Up Brilliance skills to say, 'Whoa. Let's rethink this dossier,' when we anticipate a non-approval." Imagine how much different the impact would be if he had said, "Let's do this training and then we'll see what we think — and where we might be able to use the techniques that we've learned." For this reason, we advise our clients to have application in mind and ask participants to keep a journal of how they'll use brilliance-building skills as they learn those skills.

- **A high-profile model and advocate.** We often ask a high-profile spokesperson or key executive to kick off a Lead from the Middle workshop or to host a fireside chat and say, "Here's what powering up Brilliance did for my career. Here's why I expect Brilliance of key players in our organization. Here's how I do my best to 'walk that talk.'"

- **Coaching trios.** It works for weight-loss, anger-management and smoking cessation programs, so why not build it into leadership training? When participants declare their intentions to a small group of peers who will hold them accountable — and follow-up at regular intervals — they're more likely to stay with the program and pull through the changes they've committed themselves to make.

- **Pre-post measures of success.** "We'll ask the other operations we advise to rate us with the Power Up Brilliance Readiness Survey™.," a Head of Safety announced to his team, when he kicked off the development program. "Their ratings of our group will determine whether we've met our performance objectives for the year. And your individual ratings will be used, along with technical skills, in career planning." Got your attention?

- **Concrete action plans, next steps, dates and times.** It's a risk to get specific and say, "Here's what I'll do better — by when." Insights and good intentions can go up in the ether like the New Year resolutions that you know you should do, but never make it past the Procrastination level of the Courage to Act.

- **Posters, computer wallpaper, souvenirs.** A week after a workshop that focused on improvements in Candor, a client hung elephant pictures in the conference room where the executive team met for a weekly project review. "Let's get the elephants on the table," the CEO said. Another executive, intent on fostering initiative and can-do thinking, hung a plaque in his office that said, "Our meeting will go better if you bring two solutions with every one problem."

- **An ear to the ground.** When working with leadership teams, we often check in and ask, "How's it going?" And we advise our HR partner orchestrators and executive sponsors to manage by walking around and keep "an ear to the ground" (like King Sejong and Queen Soheon, profiled in Chapter 12). If we know when participants are hitting obstacles, setbacks and conflicts, we can provide just-in-time reinforcements, after-action debriefs or huddle with individuals for pre-stresspoint rehearsals.

238

- **Sanctions, even dismissal, for imposters.** "The most brilliance-killing of all executives," one CEO told us, commenting on the challenges he faced aligning his key executives for strategy-execution, "are those who talk the talk and seem to be champions for the program, but choose entitlement over Purpose, self-protection over Risk, complacency over Will, closed-mindedness over Candor, carelessness over Rigor — when no one else on the executive team can see what they are doing and they can bully subordinates into silence." This same CEO said that he'd learned, the hard way, that there's no room on the team for those who violate trust in this way. Keeping them onboard, he said, sends a signal to everyone that undermines brilliance.

After training —mobilization and luminous efficiency

Many senior executives, like Donna, make noble efforts at Powering Up Brilliance. There was no doubt that Donna's leadership team was stuck — and that the enterprise needed bold breakthrough solutions from her department, which was responsible for the marketing function in the bank.

Donna chartered a bus, to take her entire leadership team to a two-day off-site workshop. The theme of the meeting was, "Get on the bus," with the question, "Are you all-in?" The event started as soon as the team got on board, with gameification to look at changing demographics and customer requirements; with food and drink; and with activities to lighten things up and get the team working together. It was a four hour drive to the lodge

Donna chose for the retreat. A sharp witty facilitator got "the issues" on the table, with a discussion of personality and cultural differences and the support and communications flow needed in the marketing department. Donna owned her missteps and the changes she had to make to evoke courage and foster initiative, not fear. The capstone was a day-long white water rafting trip down the Chattahoochee River. If anything could put it all together, break down barriers and Power Up Brilliance to make the team receptive to sharp critiques and fast-paced agile co-ordination, this was it.

By the time the bus returned to Corporate Headquarters, Donna's leadership team was, indeed, Powered Up. Donna smiled. This was the "wow" she had hoped for — and more. It truly looked like a new beginning. The leader was hopeful. They forgave Donna her past mistakes. Their hearts were in the right place and they were eager to get going and build on their newfound trust, communication and problem-solving skills. But the "wow" didn't last. Within less than a month, the team was back to its old dynamics — as if nothing had happened. The trip down the Chattahoochee was a joke and the metaphors were spoken about like a Dilbert cartoon. What started out as a great and auspicious beginning came crashing down, along with Donna's career and everything the bank brought her in to accomplish.

Donna's leadership program was a great success. But it failed to mobilize the team after the turn-on — and failed to Power Up Brilliance that would last. There was a huge disconnect between the Chattahoochee River and the world "back home" on the job. On the river, they had a common cause and a common antagonist — to rally them and bring them together. But

240

once that went away, the magic did not last. It was a tragic case of, "the operation was a success but the patient died."

How could Donna's team — and her consultants — have bridged that gap, between learning that is good enough in the laboratory and learning that goes a step further, from workshop to workplace? By focusing on the bus ride back to the office, even more than the bus ride out. And on what should happen in the days, weeks and months after the "turn-on," when the literal whitewater was a memory or a picture on the wall and the metaphorical whitewater — of politics, vendors, career ambitions and market forces — created real adversities for the marketing team.

Mobilization challenges workshop designers and facilitators to think beyond what we do in our e-learning games, m-learning snippets, seminar rooms, ropes courses or whitewater rafting trips, and envisage participants using the insights they learned, weeks and months later. It requires more than heartfelt discussions and personal revelations that "get tough issues out in the open" but fail to put that awareness to work. It requires us to imagine and design a springboard to action, not just a high-impact, engaging learning event. It requires what some call "Level 4 accountability" for program success — evaluating the investment not just on the basis of whether people enjoyed the experience and liked the pace and the edu-tainment — but whether they were able to achieve more brilliance faster and better, with less residual heat back on the job.

Suppose Donna's consultants had done that, and focused on team mobilization as well as teambuilding. How might they have designed the experience differently?

241

- Ask each participant to **come with a specific innovation initiative, project or challenge in mind** — that would require them to mobilize self, marketing team and external partners with a higher level of brilliance and luminous efficiency. In their book, *Rapid Results!*," Schaffer and Ashkenas (2005) advise mobilization consultants to think about the first 100 days *after* the workshop as a one-time, march-or-die opportunity to encode new skills into a leader's repertoire — and achieve quick wins that put a positive success cycle in motion.

- **Look at the team from the outside-in,** not just inside-out. Identify the partners and sponsors Donna's team needs to mobilize, to get traction on the brilliance that they want the bank to adopt. And the thought-leaders Malcolm Gladwell describes as "mavens" and "connectors" in his book, *The Tipping Point* — i.e., the trusted advisors of whom skeptical, fearful, reluctant Business Unit General Managers will ask, "Does this make sense to you? Can I entrust my career and my year-end bonus to the counter-intuitive recommendations these marketers propose?"

- **Frame the metaphors for the team,** rather than asking them to remember — and fill in the gaps for themselves. Suppose the mobilization coach had drawn parallels between the obstacles on the Chattahoochee and credibility-killers that require the team to paddle hard and in lock-step alignment, to avoid drowning in souse-holes and undercut rocks in the treacherous and turbulent political environment. "On the river," she might have said, "we anticipated the flow of the water and knew what we had to do to hit the current at exactly the right angle. Based on what we know about our champions, laggards and Luddites, what currents can we anticipate when we present our recommendations — and say, "These are the lines of business that should have the greatest visibility."

- **Build action and execution plans.** Let's face it. It's more fun — for the group and for the facilitators — to go from adventure to adventure and activity to activity, rather than taking the time to huddle and say, "Let's be specific. Who will do what by when?" It's more fun to go from case study to mindflip to insight than it is to ask, "Who do you need to approach with an uplifting dialogue?" But what's needed for learning to stick is a mix — of fun and work, insight and application, generalizations and specifics.

- **Use technology for a running start rather than a cold start.** A collaboration platform like GroupMind Express allows facilitators to open the first group discussions before the team boards the bus or enters the conference room. At a minimum, it provides a forum to share hopes and concerns. Or to assess the team's Brilliance Quotient™. Or form peer coaching trios and exchange Action Learning or Quick Results initiatives. If participants don't know each other before the workshop, it allows them to see "who's who" and go around the room (electronically) and introduce one another. And tell executives like Donna what you want from her, to lift courage and ignite brilliance in the team.

- **Pull lessons through.** Donna assumed her teambuilding work was done when the group boarded the bus for the ride home from the Chattahoochee. Mobilization assumes that's when the work shifts neutral, before going into a higher gear. A mobilization coach would have prepared Donna to bring the team together — live or via conference calls — a week after the workshop, to ask about lessons learned, lingering concerns, initial successes, setbacks already experienced that we can nip in the bud.

- **Ennoble, ennoble, ennoble.** Participants often complain that the "real world" isn't as ideal as the conditions we create for teambuilding. How true. Real life doesn't come with a facilitator or with "what's-said-in-Vegas-stays-in-Vegas" permissiveness. Real life doesn't come with every new activity giving you a fresh start. When participants complain about real-world dynamics — and say, "What can we do? It's so dysfunctional," use the skills you learned to empathize, then signal and change tracks, moving into an uplifting and ennobling, solution-focused dialogue like the one we described in Chapter 7.

- **Evaluate like you're going to the gym, not going to the theatre.** All too often, well meaning HR partners ask teambuilding participants, "How'd it go?" or "How would you rate the experience?" We agree that evaluations are essential — but "I didn't like the mannerisms of the facilitator" often becomes a justification for critics to stay stuck — and throw the lessons of the experience out, because they didn't like something about the messenger. You may not want to go home with or befriend your personal trainer at the gym, but the relevant question is, "Would you want to continue with your exercise program?" The same is true when you're building courage in a team.

A macro-design for mobilization to Power Up Brilliance

Contrast Donna's artistic success on the Chattahoochee and real-life failure on the job with a series of Power Up Brilliance workshops we conducted to with safety engineers in a fire insurance company. The engineers offered a value-added extra-charge service to large corporations who had to check that their facilities were operating in a way that complied with underwriting conditions and good risk mitigation practices. The engineers were top-grade professionals. They got high marks for customer service, operational know-how, efficiency. Everyone said they were the best in the industry. But they were losing money — lots of money — because, more than half of the time, they would show up at a customer's facility and be told, "We're right in the middle of something important. Can you wait, or come back another day? We can't afford to shut down production and allow you to inspect our equipment, electronics, fire protection and emergency procedures right now."

The workshop — the main event — included a mix of problem-solving and create-your-own-luck games, conflict-resolution and negotiation activities, diversity dialogues™ encounters, uplifting ennobling dialogues practice exercises, case studies and partnering simulations. It replicated the challenges safety engineers face, orchestrating inspections with their customers and with the Account Managers who "owned" the client relationships at the corporate level.

Within 2 months, the waste was down 50%. Within 6 months, they reduced it by 90%. It was an innovation breakthrough. They went from loss to profit, and did it without losing one single point on their customer satisfaction ratings.

We'd love to tell you that all this came as the result of a "magic bullet" in a workshop. But you know better. And so do we. Not that the workshops

The Macro-Design for Action Learning, Team Mobilization and Rapid ROI

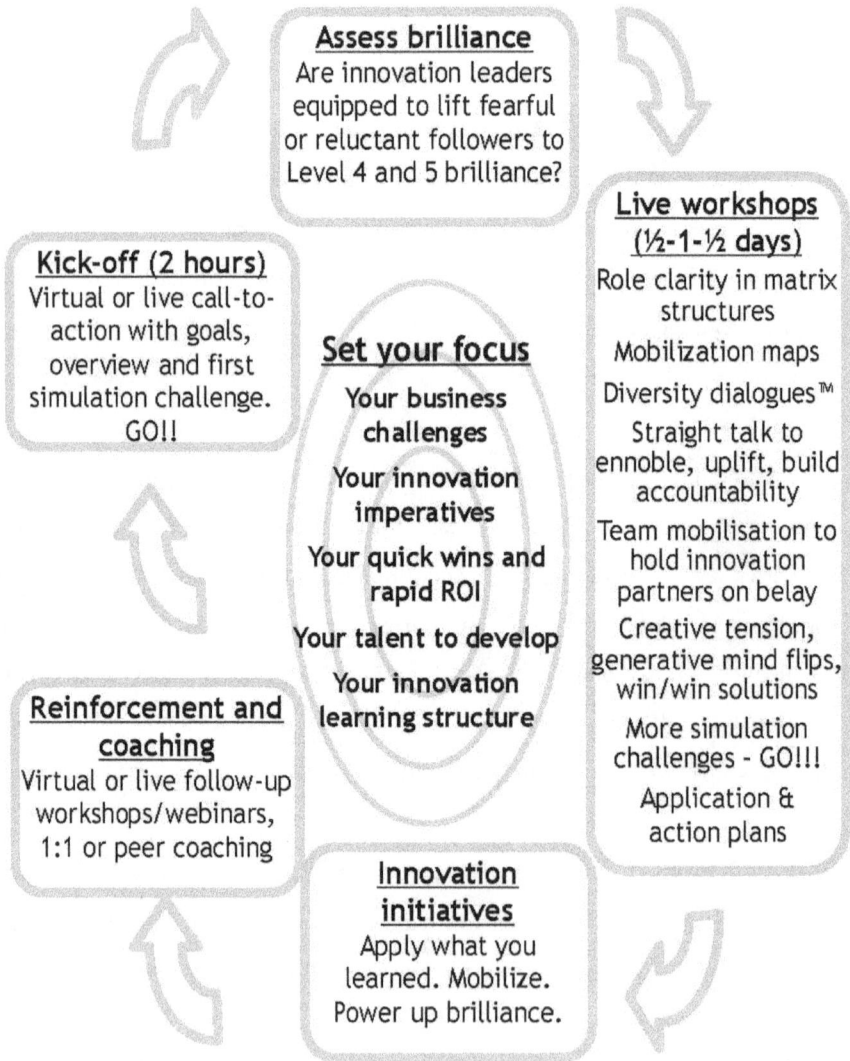

Assess brilliance
Are innovation leaders equipped to lift fearful or reluctant followers to Level 4 and 5 brilliance?

Kick-off (2 hours)
Virtual or live call-to-action with goals, overview and first simulation challenge. GO!!

Set your focus
Your business challenges
Your innovation imperatives
Your quick wins and rapid ROI
Your talent to develop
Your innovation learning structure

Live workshops (½-1-½ days)
Role clarity in matrix structures
Mobilization maps
Diversity dialogues™
Straight talk to ennoble, uplift, build accountability
Team mobilisation to hold innovation partners on belay
Creative tension, generative mind flips, win/win solutions
More simulation challenges - GO!!!
Application & action plans

Reinforcement and coaching
Virtual or live follow-up workshops/webinars, 1:1 or peer coaching

Innovation initiatives
Apply what you learned. Mobilize. Power up brilliance.

weren't engaging, vivid, paradigm-changing. They were. But ask any high-courage leader where you learn to Power Up Brilliance and they'll tell you it happens on the job, where the rubber meets the road and the lessons of the workshop meet real-life. And get traction, or not.

Team mobilization starts in the center — with the "Now What." The business justification is the focal point. It's where the compass points North, to Purpose. It's what engages the sponsors of the program, in this case, the COO responsible for engineering operations. They care less about "the art" of teambuilding than the results of mobilization. The Action Learning or Quick Results projects is where the rubber meets the road — starting, in this case, with the facilities and corporations that were the biggest money-losers, because facilities in remote locations were out of touch with corporate loss control requirements.

The cycle then moves around the clockface, starting at the 10:00 position. It's here that we go live with the participants who are learning to lift courage, in themselves and their teams. We explain key concepts — about pressure and brilliance, about orchestration roles, about the bias against creativity and other stifling forces, and about the 5 Activators — and switch on the GroupMind Express online collaboration platform.

The 12:00 position starts the exchange of ideas — with blogs, with an assessment of the team's current Brilliance Quotient™, and with a map of diverse interests and subgroups who need to be mobilized to sharpen up each other's brilliance and put it to work. Sometimes we assess the courage of each individual engineer (or orchestrator) attending the training, with

360-feedback that includes input from colleagues, sponsors, customers and workers in support roles on the team. And sometimes we'll assess the Brilliance Quotient™ of subgroups within the team — to see who needs to develop what, in order to get more leverage.

The 6:00 position is what happens after the workshop or "main event," when real task forces or account teams do real work to deliver real results in real time. It's here that it all comes together — like the golfer who finishes a masterclass, and then returns back to the home course, to use the swings that learned from the golf pro. This is where the engineers were told, "Make it happen. Get it done. Use what you've learned." And, "March or die — because failure is simply not an option."

The 8:00 position brings us full-cycle. With our safety engineers, managers watched and monitored the results. They coached for skill application. They listened, like King Sejong and Queen Soheon, and ennobled ennobled and ennobled again, lifting members of their team above fear and reluctance, denial and procrastination, blame and clumsiness — to take charge of customer relationships and account management partnerships, and find solutions that would get facilities ready for their inspections.

Fluency

When we moved to Israel, we had to be understood in a foreign language. Like many immigrants, we spoke the language in a stilted and artificial way. We learned the words, but put them together with English syntax and grammar. Patient listeners encouraged us. Impatient ones grimaced, ridiculed and even pretended not to understand what we struggled to say.

The words and syntax were hard enough to master. But they weren't the hardest part. More difficult were the mannerisms. Hebrew is a language that's spoken as much by gesture and inflection as it is by sentences and expressions. When your heart is beating in your throat and you're about to lose a small fortune in a tense negotiation, it's hard to remember to "smile when you say that" or to say something in soprano or falsetto voice, so it comes across less stern and *dugri*. It's hard to remember to step forward when you want to be taken seriously, when (according to North American standards) you're already violating the other party's personal space.

Our friends Smadar Tadmor and Kobi Rosenberg, similarly, advise leaders about fluency. Whether the leader is selling a team on "March or die" or selling a husband and wife on the design of a new kitchen sink, which is more than they wanted to spend, they're successful only if they build the courage to Power Up Brilliance. And, they also observe, we are more likely to follow someone who is fluent than someone who is stammering and unsure, who looks artificial and unnatural, and who's uncomfortable and inauthentic with courage. Fluency, Kobi and Smadar tell salespeople, means throwing the script away — so you sound like you're delivering something "from the heart," rather than giving someone a memorized spiel.

That's where practice comes in. We can give you the 5 Activators and present, as we have in this book, the science behind brilliance. We can tell you what works — and why. But the delivery — with fluency? That's where you come in. Find a way to go through the cycle that's natural and authentic — and that brings out the best of your personality? Discover what's fun and joyful — for you and the person you're ennobling? That's where you come in. And with that, we wish you "bon courage" — good success — and an uplifting ennobling friend who will encourage you and keep you on belay until you achieve fluency. With the understanding that the journey never really ends — because tomorrow's challenges, adversities, ambiguities, inflection points will test your courage yet again, and require a new infusion of Purpose, Will, Rigor, Risk and Candor.

Appendix: Assess Your Team's Brilliance Quotient™

Here are 25 questions you can ask to assess the brilliance that's powered up in a team, network or enterprise that you are mobilizing to step up, reach higher, seize new opportunities and take enterprise-success to a higher and more sustainable level.

As you read each question, think about the behavior you observe in the management board, work group, task force or enterprise you lead from the middle – as they wrestle down a thorny issue, confront an obstacle or setback or stretch to seize a particular opportunity. You'll find a scoring template for the 25 questions at the end of this Appendix (Page 266). Flag that page for easy answering — or complete this short version of the Brilliance Quotient™ online @ www.powerupbrilliance.com

Interpreting your team's Brilliance Quotient™ Profile

After you answer the 25 questions and total your scores, you'll be able to identify your team's strengths and soft spots

If you answered most of the encouraging power-up descriptors with a strong "Yes" and if your group does not erode that foundation with discouraging behavior, the chances are good that your group already fires on that cylinder.

If you answered few (or none) of the encouraging power-up descriptors with a strong "Yes" – or if your group erodes that foundation with discouraging behavior – you may need to strengthen or even rebuild that cylinder to get it to fire with the right compression under a heavy load.

For example, consider this profile of a a management team within a defense company. On a 1-6 scale, they scored high (6) on Purpose, Candor and Will, Moderate (4) on Rigor and Low (1) on Risk. What exactly does a profile like this suggest?

PURPOSE	CANDOR	WILL	RIGOR	RISK
Total Checks 1 2 3 4 5 **6**	Total Checks 1 2 3 4 5 **6**	Total Checks 1 2 3 4 5 **6**	Total Checks 1 2 3 **4**	Total Checks **1**

It tells you that they do great work when each silo in the product team is adequately resourced, equipped and informed. But when the budgets are cut and resources have to be shared or when the timelines are shortened and triage decisions need to be taken, this group does not yet have enough trust for one faction to sacrifice, share, suboptimize or or "do without," so that the entire enterprise can meet its objectives. Similarly, when decisions need to be reached by deferring to someone with enterprise-critical know-how rather than compromising to preserve harmony or consensus, there is not yet enough trust to stand back and give a "rival faction" the permission to take the lead.

As another example, consider this project team. On the same 1-6 scale, they scored high (6) on Will, Rigor and Risk, moderate (4) on Purpose and low (1) on Candor. What does this profile suggest?

PURPOSE	CANDOR	WILL	RIGOR	RISK
Total Checks 1 2 3 **4**	Total Checks **1**	Total Checks 1 2 3 4 5 **6**	Total Checks 1 2 3 4 5 **6**	Total Checks 1 2 3 4 5 **6**

This team is cordial, keeps its spirits high and is willing to support each other. They know how to orchestrate their activities, keep one another informed and adhere to quality and safety standards. But when investors, regulators, medical thought-leaders or payors set the bar higher and demand a higher standard, the team balks. They could not critique one another openly enough to say, "Here's how we can do better to achieve more aggressive goals" – or "the business case has changed and this initiative may no longer be a wise investment."

Or consider this profile, from internal auditing in a financial services company. Their investigators scored high on Rigor and Candor, moderate on Purpose and low on Will and Risk. What does this profile suggest?

PURPOSE	CANDOR	WILL	RIGOR	RISK
Total Checks 1 2 3 **4**	Total Checks 1 2 3 4 5 **6**	Total Checks **1**	Total Checks 1 2 3 4 5 **6**	Total Checks 1 **2**

They were a tough-minded, competent group who knew how to flag deviations and blow the whistle on business units that were out of compliance. But, auditing after-the-fact was no longer enough for the company to get new products on the market quickly enough to retain a competitive advantage. This group needed to step up and contribute to business objectives rather than acting as if success in the marketplace is "not our job." They needed to partner with operations rather than approaching every debate as another battle in their long-standing "we-versus-them" feud. And needed to stay mentally and emotionally engaged rather than shutting down and becoming demoralized when their risk assessments were challenged.

Now that you know how to interpret the profile from these examples, consider your own cross-functional, matrix or leadership team:

Purpose: Powered up to pursue lofty and audacious goals

Work groups with high Purpose share a compelling, clear focus that drives them all forward in the same direction. They are so inspired to accomplish the mission that they strive for optimal performance, not merely what is easy done by going after the low-lying fruit. They benchmark themselves against best-in-class or first-in-class in their industries and against breakthrough new possibilities, and pay attention to what the data tell them about how their performance measures up to that aspirational audacious standard.

1. Do they embrace a vision of success that is inspiring and compelling In Powered Up teams, colleagues can articulate why they are part of a worthwhile endeavor. They see why it is an ethical and social imperative, as well a business imperative, to stretch beyond their comfort or strike zone and optimize performance, not just try, in stepping up to make a difference.

2. Do they hold others accountable for doing their part and making solid contributions? It takes brilliance to look performance data in the eye and say, "Here's what we need to do better" rather than "Here's why it wasn't our fault – or why it should not matter." In Powered Up teams, people hold themselves and their colleagues accountable for success not merely "trying hard" or "doing what they are told to do."

3. Do they exhibit business acumen to know what it takes to be competitive? They figure out why some things contribute more to enterprise-success than others, even if no one explains it explicitly. They set priorities based on what is best for the enterprise, not merely "who shouts loudest" or "who wields the most power."

4. Do they keep innovation efforts focused on breakthroughs that will deliver solid business results? It takes brilliance to look beyond achievable incremental improvements and old trendlines and embrace aspirations that are audacious. In Powered Up teams, members of the group understand why the bar is set

255

higher – and how the competitive landscape is changing. They use valid benchmarks to assess their performance and challenge themselves to reach or exceed parity – or sustain their position as market leaders.

5. Do they settle for incremental improvements by missing opportunities or doing the wrong things? In fearful or complacent teams, people confine their efforts to the things they like to do at a pace that they find comfortable and easy. They do not jump until everyone feels ready and do not ask people to do jobs that are beneath them, above them or that they would prefer not to do. They focus on technology or scientific pursuits that are "cool" and artistically fulfilling, with only a vague notion how it impacts the business. It may feel good for people to stay within the comfort, curiousity or security zones but, as a result, they find out later than promising opportunities have passed them by – as customers, investors or payors seek other alternatives.

Candor: Powered up to speak and hear the truth

When Candor is alive and well on a team, the members speak freely and share ideas and insights, feelings and needs. Tough issues are faced straight-on, and feedback is delivered in a tactful and timely manner. The result is a climate of openness and non-defensiveness in which what needs to be said is said in a manner that can be heard. Members of the team say what needs to be said; they also report that they feel heard and respected by those around them.

1. Do they solicit input from people with diverse backgrounds and perspectives? It takes brilliance to go looking for contrary evidence, alternative points of view and to operate with transparency when you might be inviting criticism. It is far more comfortable to talk with people who see things the way you do and will confirm your conclusions, praise your work and endorse your recommendations. Groups with Candor don't just accept feedback from people who see things differently; they actively reach out and seek input from people who speak different languages, represent minority groups and need an invitation to speak up and get involved.

2. Do they address fears, doubts and skepticism? It takes brilliance to empathize with the concerns that are real to someone else, rather than trivializing or delegitimizing their worries. Groups with Candor listen carefully and explore disagreements, without politicizing conflicts or getting locked into adversarial positions. They use humor to modulate tension, lighten things up and get people to take issues seriously without taking themselves too seriously.

3. Do they welcome a robust debate to pressure-test proposals and formulate the best possible solution? Yes, it takes brilliance to hear opposition and criticism, and to take feedback on board without trying to neutralize or overcome opposition. And to assert what you need to do your job well and make your best contributions. It takes brilliance to refine or revise your plans — and to consider counter-intuitive ideas, risks and experiences (backed up with data, of course) that are different from those of your own age group, nationality or profession.

4. Do they use humor and a spirit of appreciative inquiry to de-politicize contentious issues? It takes brilliance to speak up and break silence when there is collusion to "go along to get along." To break the grip of icy stares and political expediency, and tell higher-ups about risk factors that they would like to power through or wish away. And to do it in a way that is appreciative of the goals that sponsors are trying to accomplish and the leaps of faith you are asking them to take, in a way that builds trust.

5. Do they enable others to make excuses and avoid personal accountability? Fearful or complacent groups are superficially nice, polite, accepting. There's a "go-along-to-get-along" norm of permissiveness when agreements are violated, timelines breached, budgets blown, quality or safety standards compromised. People are dismissed as being "too demanding" or "difficult personalities" if they ask tough questions, offer ideas, assert their needs, enforce contract provisions or provide feedback that could be unsettling.

Will: Powered Up to inspire optimism, hope and spirit

Teams with a strong will believe in themselves. They have a "fire in their belly," a belief that their hard work and good intentions will, ultimately, pay off. Will is a can-do, make-it-happen attitude that renews energy. When a team has this resilience, people feel it and, in its best form, they are optimistic that they can rise to any challenge and accomplish almost anything.

1. Do they energize colleagues and lift their spirits? Pay attention to the tone, spirit and energy that people project to one another, in email exchanges, teleconferences and face-to-face exchanges. Do people exude enthusiasm when they write or talk about their work? Smile? Attitudes are contagious; in groups with the will to succeed, people project an upbeat, positive attitude that sweeps others up in their energy.

2. Do they show pride about seeing everyone do their personal best? Brilliance is joyful – when team members take pride in what they're accomplishing, whether it's finding an elegant solution to a vexing problem, moving a business development effort to the next level, facilitating a productive meeting, cementing a partnership. People talk in positive terms about their colleagues and their managers, even when there are obstacles and problems to solve. They egg one another on and challenge one another to be the best that they can be. When they talk informally, they look and sound like they put their heart into the job – rather than being blasé or just going through the motions.

3. Do they inspire a resourceful "can-do" attitude about uncertainty and adversity? Strong-willed groups are self-starting and its members believe they have the capacity to solve their own problems. They thrive on the challenge of the problem solving rather than stopping in their tracks altogether or waiting passively until higher-ups to direct. If they make mistakes, it's a mistake of going too far too fast, rather than the mistake of sitting and doing nothing. There's a work hard/play hard feel to a team that's always looking for better ideas, upgraded methods, breakthrough possibilities.

4. Do they convey a sense of urgency? You can feel the rhythm, the G-force acceleration, the energy in a strong-willed team. The pace is fast. Time is measured not only by clocks and calendars, but by a cadence that says, "Now." They walk (and write) with a bounce in their step and do whatever they can to pick up the pace, in themselves and the other matrix partners they mobilize.

5. Do they get upset or de-energized by setbacks or complications? In fearful or complacent teams, people are stuck or discouraged when the going gets tough. They focus on "what went wrong" and "who's to blame" -- on the threat of impending catastrophe, more than what can be done to course-correct and seize new opportunities. When some people take charge and jump into action, you can feel their fear, their gloom-and-doom crisis scenarios, and the shockwaves they send with implied or stated threats.

Rigor: Powered Up to invent, refine and stick to best practices

Rigor involves a respect for the methods, routines, and protocols necessary to keep the team and its members on track. It is a step beyond good intentions and represents the institutionalizing of practices that insure greater discipline to the process of how work is accomplished. In a fast-paced and agile business environment, Rigor ensures safety, regulatory compliance and prevents expensive or embarrassing miscommunications and miscalculations. And finds and encodes breakthrough solutions.

1. Do they stay current on the very best and latest techniques and know-how? In rigorous groups, people are alert for the experts who know more, learn and problem-solve faster. They are eager to find out more about the best solutions and best practices, including those that were "not invented here" or that were proposed by other departments or rival teams. They recruit colleagues who are smarter and more knowledgeable than they are – rather than feeling threatened by that know-how.

2. Do they take advantage of forums for out-of-the-box thinking and idea-generation? In rigorous teams, planning and idea-generating forums are used to pressure-test ideas, find innovative possibilities, accelerate one another's work. Blogs, online forums, informal huddles and formal planning meetings generate better and better ideas. Budgets and timelines are vehicles to accelerate progress and achieve more with less capital; not just to compile ideas into a bureaucratic or administrative overview.

3. Do they adopt new better practices that ensure safety, quality, sustainability, compliance? In rigorous groups, people know their jobs, their equipment, regulations and specifications well enough to know what ensures a job well done. They not only monitor their own work; in addition, they pay attention to what others are doing – both in their own location and other locations – to ensure adherence to quality and regulatory standards.

4. Do they establish robust mechanisms for co-ordination and planning? In rigorous groups, people working in one pod of activity anticipate their impact on other groups working upstream and downstream from them — and in parallel activities. They reach out and co-ordinate, both in the hand-offs they make with work products and equipment and in the way they communicate and share information.

5. Do they use short-cuts that adversely affect the productivity of others? In fearful or complacent teams, things may not look "ship-shape" when you open supply cabinets and databases, review logs or scratch below the surface. People may be so busy doing work that they invest little in preventive maintenance. If you ask for a report, for inventory or a piece of equipment, they may not know how to retrieve it quickly, with a minimum of hunting and searching. All of these are mistakes, liabilities or accidents waiting to happen – or inefficiencies and extra work caused by a narrow or short-term focus, where people do not know enough beyond their own department or pod of activity to see how their work impacts others.

Risk: Powered Up to trust others and invest in relationships

In matrix structures and alliances, success requires people to share information and resources, work together and deploy talent and resources in a way that will optimize enterprise-wide performance, rather than one's own individual or work group performance. Risk revolves around relationships, cooperation and support – reflected in what people do, not just the image they try to put forward. With Risk, teammates are willing to make themselves vulnerable to support one another, go the extra mile for one another, and entrust their success to someone else's actions. Trust is what makes this possible.

1. Do they trust others to make good independent decisions? Empowerment is a risk. In trusting groups, stakeholders trust the judgment of others, rather than demanding a seat at the table to protect their own self-interests. They trust others enough to proxy their influence — rather than second-guessing decisions or agreements that they did not negotiate personally.

2. Do they help others get the information, resources or opportunities they need? It takes trust to notice what a colleague needs and to offer them resources or information before being asked to share – or directed to "give it up" by someone with the authority to adjudicate or rationalize capacity. Flat matrix structures and alliances only work if stakeholders operate with this kind of trust.

3. Do they affirm the good intentions and competence of people who inconvenience them? In high-trust groups, people give each other benefit of the doubt when they experience a delay, a last-minute request, a change in priorities or some other inconvenience. When setbacks or mistakes occur, they create learning and growth opportunities – and resolve misunderstandings in a way that deepens trust.

4. Do they encourage others to improvise and take initiative? In high-trust teams, orchestrators give colleagues latitude to use judgment and discretion rather than insisting that everything be done 'by the book' and micro-managing.

5. Do they fulfill personal ambitions and agendas before helping others? In groups with trust, people are will delay gratification or will take a "hit" for the good of the team. They describe their enterprise with pronouns like "we" and "us" rather than "you" and "them." They have their egos and ambitions under control and understand that no one succeeds unless everyone succeeds. They allow someone else to stand in the spotlights and get accolades and glory, understanding that only one lead actor or producer will stand on the podium and accept an Academy Award. In fearful or complacent teams, people are more concerned with protecting their own self-interests rather than putting enterprise-success ahead of personal success

What does this tell you about the brilliance that is Powered Up in your matrix or support network?

As you answer the 25 questions, chart your YES and NO answers here — to see the strengths and weaknesses when you Power Up Brilliance in your team. Give your team one check for each YES on questions 1 to 4, and give your network two checks if you can give question 5 a strong NO.

Those that are heavily laden with checkmarks are the strongest Activators. Those that have the most blanks are the Activators you need to improve, whether you are leading from the middle-out, the bottom-up or the top-down, to Power Up Brilliance in your network.

5 ACTIVATORS: SCORE THESE 25 QUESTIONS

PURPOSE	CANDOR	WILL	RIGOR	RISK
1. Yes __	1. Yes __	1. Yes __	1. Yes __	1. Yes __
2. Yes __	2. Yes __	2. Yes __	2. Yes __	2. Yes __
3. Yes __	3. Yes __	3. Yes __	3. Yes __	3. Yes __
4. Yes __	4. Yes __	4. Yes __	4. Yes __	4. Yes __
5. No __ (twice) __	5. No __ (twice) __	5. No __ (twice) __	5. No __ (twice) __	5. No __ (twice) __
Total Checks 1 2 3 4 5 6	Total Checks 1 2 3 4 5 6	Total Checks 1 2 3 4 5 6	Total Checks 1 2 3 4 5 6	Total Checks 1 2 3 4 5 6

Refererences

Bardwick, JM (1995). *Danger in the comfort zone: From boardroom to mailroom how to break the entitlement habit that is killing American business.* New York: AMACOM.

Ben-Shahar, T. (2007). *Happier: Learn the secrets to daily joy and lasting fulfillment.* New York: McGraw Hill.

Bent, K (2011). *The decline of Blackberry:* Where RIM went wrong. San Francisco (USA): CRN: News, analysis and perspective for VARs and technology integrators.

Birkman, RW. (1995). *True colours: Understand yourself and others better.* Nashville TN (USA): Thomas Nelson.

Boyd, D & Goldenberg, J (2013). *Inside the box: A proven system of creativity for breakthrough results.* New York: Simon and Schuster.

Brafman, O & Beckstrom, RA. (2008). *The starfish and the spider. The unstoppable power of leaderless organizations.* New York: Penguin Books.

Briggs, KC and Myers, IB. (1948) *Myers Briggs Type Indicator.* Mountain View CA (USA): Consulting Psychologists Press

Cooke, R & Szumal, J (1993). *Life Styles Inventory (LSI).* Ann Arbor MI (USA): Human Synergistics.

Davis, H & Davis, D (2005). *Israel in the world: Changing lives through Innovation.* London (UK): Weidenfeld & Nicolson

De Bono, E (1999). *Six thinking hats.* New York: Back Bay Books.

Edgett, SJ & Cooper, RG (2012). *Generating breakthrough new product ideas: Feeding the innovation funnel.* Guelph: Product Development Institute.

Frohman, D & Howard, R. (2008). *Leadership the hard way: Why leadership can't be taught and how you can learn it anyway.* San Francisco (USA): Jossey-Bass

Fung, VK; Fung, WK & Wind, YR (2007). *Competing in a flat world: Building enterprises for a borderless world.* Upper Saddle River NJ (USA): Prentice Hall.

Geier, JG (1975). DISC personality profile system. St Paul MN (USA): Performax.

Gerstein, MS & Shaw, R (2009). Organizational bystanders. *People + strategy.* 31:1, pp 47- 54.

Gilder, G & Lieberman, J (2012). *The Israel test. Why the worlds most besieged state is a beacon of freedom and hope for the world economy.* New York (USA): Encounter Books.

Gittell, JH (2009). *The Southwest Airlines way: Using the power of relationships to achieve high performance.* New York: McGraw Hill.

Gladwell, M (2011). *Outlyers: The story of success.* New York (USA): Back Bay Books.

Godin, S (2012 *dec*). *The Icarus eption: How high will you fly?* New York (USA): Portfolio Penguin.

Goldratt, E; Cox, J & Whitford, D (2012). *The goal: A process of ongoing improvement (Rev ed).* Great Barrington MA(USA): Great River Press.

Gore, A (2007). *The assault on reason.* New York (USA): Penguin Press.

Harvey, J (1988). *The abilene paradox and other meditations on management.* San Francisco (USA): Jossey-Bass.

Hofstede, G; Hofstede, GJ & Minkov, M. (2010). *Cultures and organizations: Software of the mind (3rd edition).* New York (USA): McGraw Hill.

IBM Corporation (2010). *Capitalizing on complexity: Insights from the Global Chief Executive Officer study.* Somers NY (USA): IBM Global Business Services.

Isaacson, W (2011). *Steve Jobs.* New York (USA): Simon and Shuster.

Katzenbach, J (2010). *Leading outside the lines: How to mobilize the informal organization, energize your team and get better results.* San Francisco (USA): Jossey

Bass.

Klein, G (2011). *Streetlights and shadows: Searching for the keys to adaptive decision-making.* Boston (USA): MIT Press.

Klein, G (1999). *Sources of power: How people make decisions.* Boston (USA): MIT Press.

Klein, G (2004). *The power of intuition: How to use your gut instincts to make better decisions at work.* Boston (USA): MIT Press.

Klein, MI & Napier, RA. (2003) *The courage to act: 5 factors of courage to transform business.* London (UK): Nicholas-Brealey.

Knudson, L (2013). Generating Leaders, GE Style. HR Management.

Kotter, J (2012). *Leading change.* Boston (USA): Harvard Business Review Press.

Krames, JA (2005). *Jack Welch and the 4 Es of leadership.* New York (USA): McGraw Hill.

Leung, R (2009). The mench of Malden Mills New York (USA): CBS 60 Minutes News.

McCain, J. (2008). *Why courage matters. The way to a braver life.* New York (USA): Ballentine Books.

McKee, A & Boyatzis, RE (2008). *Becoming a resonant leader: Develop your emotional intelligence, renew your relationships, sustain your effectiveness.* Boston (USA): Harvard Business Review Press.

McKinney, P (2012). *Beyond the obvious: Killer questions that spark game-changing innovation.* New York (USA): Hyperion.

Mueller, JS; Melwani, S & Concalo, JA (2011). *The bias against creativity: Why people desire but reject creative ideas.* Ithica NY (USA): Cornell University ILR School.

Napier, R. (2013). *Seduction of the leader.* In press.

Napier, R & Gershenfeld, M (2004). *Groups: Theory and experience (7th edition).* Boston (USA): Houghton-Mifflin.

Napier, R & Gershenfeld, M (1999). *Advanced games for trainers.* New York: McGraw Hill.

Napier, R & McDaniel R (2006). *Measuring what matters: Simplified tools for aligning teams and their stakeholders.* London (UK): Nicholas Brealey.

Napier, R; Sidle, C & Sanaghan, P (1997). *High impact tools and activities for strategic planning: Creative techniques for facilitating your organization's planning process.* New York: McGraw Hill.

Nili, R; Goldberg, H; Weizman, A & Dudal, Y (of Weizman Institute, Israel). Fear thou not: Activity of frontal and temporal circuits in moments of real-life courage. *Neuron,* 2010 (June). 66 (6): 949-962.

Odwyn, M & Gittell, JH (2011). Sociology of organizations: Structures and relationships. Thousand Oaks CA (USA): SAGE Publications.

Oshry, B (2007). *Seeing systems: Unlocking the mysteries of organizational life.* San Francisco (USA): Berrett-Kohler.

Pascale, R; Sternin, J & Sternin, M (2010). *The power of positive deviance: How unlikely innovators solve the worlds toughest problems.* Boston (USA): Harvard Business Review Press.

Prokesch, S (2009). How GE teaches teams to lead change. Boston (USA): Harvard Business Review.

Rosenberg, M & Silvert, D (2012). *Taking flight: Master the DISC styles to transform your career, your relationships, your life.* Upper Saddle River NJ (USA): FT Press.

Rosenthal, R & Jacobson, L (2003). *Pygmalion in the classroom: Teacher expectations and pupils' intellectual development.* New York (USA): Crown House Publishing.

Sanaghan, P & Napier, R (2002). *Interional design and the process of change.* Washington DC (USA): Nucubo.

Sarnack, J (2012). *ImagineNation.* Zichron Yaakov: ImagineNation.

Seligman, MEP (1998). *Learned optimism: How to change your mind and your life.* New York (USA): Simon and Shuster Penguin Press, 1998.

Seligman, MEP (2003). *Authentic happiness: Using the new positive psychology to realize your potential for lasting fulfillment.* New York (USA): Simon and Shuster Free Press.

Senor, D & Singer, S (2011). *Startup nation: The story of Israel's economic miracle.* New York: Twelve.

Sheppard, H ª1975). *Rules of thumb for change agents.* Cambridge MA (USA): Herb Sheppard Foundation.

Silverstein, J (2009). Panel discussion on the future of life science discovery research, Biomed Conference, Tel Aviv.

Snell, GR & Moussa, M (2007). *The art of woo: Using strategic persuasion to sell your ideas.* New York (USA): Penguin Books.

Storm, H (1972). *Seven arrows.* New York: Ballentine Books.

Watkins, M (2003). *The first 90 days: Critical success strategies for new leaders at all levels.* Boston (USA): Harvard Business Review Press.

Weisbord, M & Janoff, S (2010). *Future search: Getting the whole system in the room for vision, commitment and action.* San Francisco (USA): Berrett-Koehler.

Wind, YR & Cook, C (2006). *The power of impossible thinking: Transform the business of your life and the life of your business.* Upper Saddle River NJ (USA): Pearson Education Prentice Hall.

Wiseman, R. (2004). *The luck factor: The four essential principals.* London (UK): Miramax Books.

Zintz, A & Jones C (2011). *Adaptive inquiry.* Pennington NJ (USA): Strategic Leadership Resources.

www.ingramcontent.com/pod-product-compliance
Lightning Source LLC
Chambersburg PA
CBHW021919190326
41519CB00009B/849